The Sound of a Miracle

The Sound of a Miracle

A Child's Triumph over Autism

Annabel Stehli

Published by The Georgiana Institute, Inc.
Roxbury, CT 06783

Distributed by Midpoint Trade Books

Copyright © 1991 by Annabel Stehli

PUBLISHING HISTORY
Doubleday hardcover edition / 1991
Avon paperback edition / 1992
First Georgiana Institute Printing / 1996

Library of Congress Cataloging-in-Publication Data
The sound of a miracle : a child's triumph over autism / by
Annabel Stehli—1st ed.
p. cm.
1. Stehli, Georgie—Mental health.
2. Autistic children—United States—Biography.
3. Autistic children—United States—Family relationships.
I. Title.
362.1'98928982'0092—dc 20   90–37456
ISBN 0-9644838-1-5

2 4 6 8 10 9 7 5 3

Printed in the United States of America

To Georgie,
for her courage and determination

Acknowledgments

With special thanks to Anne Edelstein, my agent, and Casey Fuetsch, my editor. Others who were particularly helpful were Shelby Howatt, Sophy Burnham, Bernard Rimland, Celestine Frost, Virginia Blaker, Joan Matthews, and my mother, Claudia Hatch. I would also like to thank Marianne Bell, Anne Pratt, Lee Kneerim, Jill Scott, Tom and Lee Ann Newcomb, Mary Dauman, Bill and Mary Ann Hall, Lee and Elane Richardson, Doris Chiappetta, Margo Lyon Nemeth, the Caravaglia family, Jacky Brown, Bill Brown, Peggy Kingsbury, Pat Stone, Henry and Susan von Maur, Eileen Fletcher, Glenna Smith, Courtney Davis, Katharine, Joan, and Gordon Younce, Vreni Merriam, Sue Brainerd, Alison Brook, Julie Mudge, Jackie Glass, Bob Weeks, Mary Calahan, Hope and Brad Anschutz, Mary Klee, Roberta Kyle, Betsy Grant, Kitty Stehli, Tom and Naomi Hatch, Aunt Pat Haines, David and Carol Stearns, Georgia Harbison, John Stearns, and Reinhart and Gisela Fischer, and Beth Hume.

In the interest of protecting the privacy of certain people whose real identities are not essential to this true account, some names have been changed.

Contents

Contents

Part One

Chapter 1

Inklings

"It feels like a knife cutting through cream cheese," I said to the doctor as she wielded her scalpel on my stomach. It was May 24, 1965, and I was a scared twenty-five-year-old in the hospital having an emergency cesarean section. Because I'd had breakfast an hour and a half earlier, they hadn't given me general anesthesia.

A saddle block had numbed me from the waist down, and although I'd always wanted to witness an operation, I'd never dreamed the first one I'd see would be my own. Since I'd had problems holding on to the baby, I'd known I might have to have a cesarean, but I hadn't contemplated being awake. No mirror was provided, but I could see myself reflected in the glass of a large light over the table, and it was fascinating to watch the blade as it cleaved my stomach, and dark-looking blood seeped up.

I was having my second child a month early because I'd had a "partial placenta previa," where the edge of the placenta, the lining of the uterus which supplies the baby with nutrients and oxygen, partially obstructs the entrance to the womb. Often hemorrhaging and oxygen deprivation (anoxia) result. When the first episode of bleeding occurred, I was barely into my eighth month, and was rushed to the hospital, where I remained flat on my back for three weeks to give the baby a chance to grow to term. As term approached, I was allowed to go home to wait for labor to begin. Three days later, I bled again and had to be readmitted. This time the doctor advised an immediate cesarean, as she thought that perhaps 20 percent of the placenta was now missing and there was a risk of further bleeding. She was particularly concerned about the possibility of anoxia. "The baby might be compromised," she said. I wished I'd never had to hear that sentence.

My first baby had been delivered with no problem. Her name was Dotsie, and she was now a stocky, cute, and lively two-year-old, with pink cheeks and thick blond hair cut like a Dutch boy's. I could picture her at home playing on the floor with her blocks. She was the kind of kid who looked great in red overalls. My husband, Bill, would be with her, staying out of the way, as fathers usually did in the days before natural childbirth. He would probably be reading the paper and having a cup of coffee while she played, sitting in our brownstone apartment in Brooklyn Heights, with the sun streaming in the windows.

This second baby was one we'd planned, but we'd been worried. We hadn't had much chance to get used to each other before our first baby arrived, and we hoped we could handle the responsibility another one would involve. Our problem was that we were incurable romantics, and when we'd had to sell our MG, our motor scooter, *and* our folding kayak which we kept in the closet, in order to pay for babies, we had minded more than we should have. Responsibilities were weighing heavily, and we had to admit, when we were honest, that our first year together had been our best.

I was in twelfth grade in New York and Bill was a student at Columbia when we first started seeing each other, and although I had considered him irresistible, I'd had no business even thinking about going out with him. I was a naïve, impressionable, idealistic seventeen-year-old, and he was a jaded and glamorous older man of twenty-four, of whom my parents didn't approve. But when I met him, I decided he was "the one."

On an April afternoon in 1956, my brother David and I were driving along East Eighty-sixth Street in Manhattan when David spotted Bill striding along on his way to his building on the corner. He was a former classmate who had just gotten back from Korea, and when David yelled a greeting, Bill turned and stopped. He was tall, tanned, and elegant, with brown hair combed straight back, a thin Roman nose, turquoise blue eyes, and a perfect smile. When he came over to the car, he leaned down to say hello to David and his face was only inches from mine.

It took me four months of subtle and ingenious flirting before he asked me out, and soon after that we were together every weekday morning for coffee before school, both evenings of the weekend, and on the telephone every weeknight as well. It was a miracle that I managed to get into the college of my choice. He took me to Chinese restaurants with a sophisticated Chinese friend who ordered up incredible delicacies in dictatorial Chinese, he taught me to use chopsticks and to love Japanese food as well, he introduced me to a group of older, creative people who intrigued me, and every Saturday night he took me dancing at the Stork Club. It was the dancing that was the greatest lure. He took a very strong lead, danced like a professional, and knew every step of every ballroom dance. We became part of the entertainment at the Stork Club, often monopolizing the floor and drawing applause for our terpsichorean flamboyance and expertise. We were usually at it every Saturday night from nine o'clock until we closed the place.

Except on the dance floor, where we rarely talked, there were problems from the beginning, clashes of values in particular, and we fought and broke up many times. I lost twenty pounds, from sheer nervousness more than excitement, because I could never be quite sure of him; yet we were extremely attached to each other. When I went away to Nantucket the summer I was eighteen, and became friends with someone closer to me in age who was going into the ministry, I realized that a crucial element of trust had been missing from Bill's and my relationship, and that I was going to have to end it. Bill couldn't understand how I could do such a thing since he'd never done anything untrustworthy, and I didn't know how to explain, because it was just a feeling. But I said good-bye and didn't think I'd ever see him again.

I went off to college, and he dropped out of college and moved to Charleston, South Carolina, where he had friends. He enjoyed his life there, working at a clerical job at the port authority, singing in a choir, playing on the town baseball team, and dancing in the city ballet company, where he played all the villains although he'd never had a lesson in his life. But after three years, his father talked him into coming back to New York to make some real money, and Bill went to work in the brokerage business.

He and my brother had remained friends, so we were bound to meet at some point. When we did, we were both lonely and struggling to find ourselves, and stuck in "respectable" jobs we didn't really want. Everyone we knew started getting married, and suddenly it had seemed like a good idea since we knew each other so well and liked to be together all the time. And when we hadn't been able to bring each other as much happiness as we'd expected, we were advised by friends and family to grow up and lower our standards: happy marriage was an oxymoron and a bromide for the unrealistic in this world. I tried to jump through his mother's hoops, and become a glossy, sophisticated, ultrapolite ladylike young married person who was awfully good at decorating, when what I really wanted to be was a bohemian writer and actress. Bill tried to become a stellar provider, and a righteous, sober fellow, when he would much rather have been painting in SoHo and subsisting on absinthe and sukiyaki.

Coexisting with our romantic hidden agendas was the urge to have financial security and success. We were the first to admit that we were "crazy mixed-up kids" but had no idea how to begin to sort our lives out. Bill believed everything would fall into place when he made his pile and could quit and become an artist. I believed— although we couldn't have afforded one—that a shrink was probably what I needed. My mother agreed. She had been the Dear Abby of the teenage world for *Seventeen* magazine, answering thousands of letters every month. She worked in tandem with a psychiatrist who became her guru, and she had taught me everything there was to know about the id, the libido, and the superego. Psychiatry had become her religion, with Freud, Jung, and Adler its patron saints, and she held the conviction that the key to happiness lay in resolving childhood conflicts. Bill, however, was anti-therapy, having doubtless also been influenced by his mother. She believed in good luck, good manners, and common sense (as well as the three B's, of course—background, breeding, and boarding school). Bill said, "I don't know why you need a shrink when you analyze everything anyway all by yourself." It was true that I loved to pick everything apart in a relentless effort to figure out what was really going on. I could never take anything at face value, and justified it by saying it was my writer's mentality, a mentality that was ridiculed by my husband's family, who relegated writers to the leprous ranks of the rude and traitorous.

When Betty Friedan's *The Feminine Mystique* was published in 1963, the year Dotsie was born, it became my emancipation proclamation and gave me a handle on my unhappiness, which I now thought I could do something about. "That's what's wrong here," I said, and proclaimed myself an enslaved housewife with no name, owned by my master, doomed to a life of unpaid domestic service, lured by a ring, a wedding, and the legalized promise of security, sold into slavery by my father when he "gave me away," and trapped by lack of personal funds and paid holidays and vacations. I would have a few drinks at a party and get up on my soapbox and rail about the lot of the poor housewife, announcing that I was writing a play about a housewives' strike organized through daytime TV that would bring a nation of male chauvinists to its knees. The saying "Man's work ends with the setting sun, women's work is never done" upset me. And yet I adored my baby and had from the first instant, and wanted to be a happy, healthy, positive mother and a good wife. It was confusing, living on the cusp of a new era, and I didn't know how to handle it.

Since my mother had always worked and had found it fulfilling and exciting, I decided that the only solution was to get a job. For six months I free-lanced at home evaluating applications for an international scholarship program, the work I'd done before I was married. Then, when Dotsie was eight months old, I found a babysitter and went to work for CBS. My evenings and weekends with my daughter became such a pleasure that after a year or so, nothing seemed more right and important than having another baby.

The advent of this second child, however, had made me wonder if staying home wasn't the answer after all. "You couldn't leave *two* with a sitter, you'd miss them too much," I told myself. And I took myself to task. "If other people find fulfillment in it, why can't you?" What I really wanted was to stay home and keep the sitter too, but since that would be having my cake and eating it too, I chided myself for acting immature. I became more and more determined to find a way to become "just a housewife" and do it justice. I found myself envying uneducated, bovine women who took it all in stride and gloried in seeing their faces reflected in their clean, shining plates.

After a few months I was restless again, and although I spent most of my time taking care of Dotsie, I got a free-lance assignment from a publishing company to do a "nonbook book" for teenagers, consisting of a weekly calendar with proverbs and quizzes. It wasn't *War and Peace*, but at least I had a book contract which referred to me as an "author"; my name was going to be on the cover, and it was a start.

I enjoyed the mornings I spent in the library each week while Dotsie was in her play group, digging out gems like "Triumph is merely umph added to try" and "He who refuses praise seeks praise twice." Because the proverbs had to be wholesome and nonreligious, it took months to find fifty-two of them, and I found it fascinating to do the research, my short-form philosophy course I called it. In addition, it gave us some extra money and made the hours I spent with Dotsie more enjoyable because it diluted my focus.

When Dotsie became a toddler, she was the busy kind, and rampaged all over our apartment, pulling over lamps, taking books out of the bookcases, emptying drawers, even getting into the ashes in the fireplace. I had read everything from Spock to Montessori,

and didn't want to interfere with her need to master her environment, but I felt she had to have *some* discipline. She was highly
resistant to it, though, and I would stand there sometimes and watch
her on what I called her search-and-destroy missions, thinking this
too shall pass, and looking forward to nursery school. Her saving
grace was that she was, of course, the cutest, cuddliest little girl I'd
ever seen, and also, I loved the way she talked. Starting out with
streams of jargon, now she'd progressed to saying "bessie" for
sweater, "zacket" for jacket, and "modogassy" for motor scooter.
And once, when she was looking out the window in her bedroom,
she said, "Look, Mommy, birdie walkin' in de sky." When I had
tried to add another little person to the scene in my mind—a wiggly
little baby sister or brother for Dotsie—it seemed too miraculous
to imagine. But I loved the thought of it and made yellow flowered
bumpers for the family cradle by hand, in anticipation.

I watched spellbound as the doctor folded back the layers of my
stomach lining in preparation for delivering the baby. She was apprehensive. Not only had I had problems with the pregnancy, but
it had taken her over an hour and a half this morning to locate the
anesthesiologist, during which time I had been lying in a little holding room worrying about anoxia and possible brain damage to the
baby, and agonizing over how long it was taking to arrange for this
"emergency procedure."

"Here we go," she said as she grasped a tiny, slippery shoulder.
Within seconds, the baby was cradled in her hands, perfectly formed
and fast asleep. "You've got yourself another girl." A nurse took the
baby and suctioned mucus from her nose and mouth. I held my
breath when she made no sound. They held her by her feet and
spanked her with staccato little slaps that stood out in the quiet like
BB shots until, finally, there was a thin, feeble cry.

When she was weighed, the doctor said, "She's five pounds six
ounces. More than I thought but she'll still have to be in an incubator
for two days because she's premature by two ounces. It's state law."

"Can I hold her?" I asked.

"She has to be cleaned off and then she has to go into the incubator." Quietly, thinking I wouldn't hear her, she said to a nurse who was standing nearby, "She has a low Apgar score." But my oversensitive hearing picked it up like a blip on a radar screen.

"What's an Apgar score?" I knew, but I asked anyway, hoping I was wrong.

"It's a rating system for the baby, but you weren't supposed to hear that. Don't worry about it, it's probably nothing. Now you're just supposed to relax, so I'm going to give you something to knock you out while I sew you up."

It hadn't been the kind of birth where everyone felt a rush of triumph, there had been something muted and covert about it, and I knew something was wrong. But before I had a chance to protest, I was given a shot, and mercifully drifted off.

I woke up hours later, sore and miserable, asking for the baby, but was told I couldn't see her because she was still in the incubator. I was in so much pain, and was so emotionally drained by the thought that something was wrong, that I couldn't argue forcefully.

My pediatrician was brusque and evasive when I questioned her. I wondered if she was in cahoots with my obstetrician, whom I wasn't sure I trusted anymore. With my authority figures wobbling on their pedestals, I looked to myself. I began to obsess about something which I thought must have triggered the placenta previa in the first place. It had occurred a few months before when Dotsie and I had gone to the playground. Now, the image stood out vividly in my mind.

It was a cold, blustery March day, not long after Dotsie's second birthday. The sky was overcast and the wind off the harbor cut through our parkas, whistling around the corners of buildings and snapping up litter from the sidewalk. I'd wrapped Dotsie like a papoose in our red plaid steamer rug, and she sat immobile in her stroller, squinting to keep out the cold. In this weather, we didn't want to walk the seven long blocks to the cheerful, crowded playground on Pierrepont Street where we usually went and, instead, opted for what we called the deserted playground. It was nearby, but it was a lonely half-acre of concrete surrounded by a gray metal fence, laid out in the shadow of the elevated Brooklyn-Queens Expressway. As we approached it, I checked for unsavory figures lurking behind the steel supports of the highway, and could see the gray water of the harbor through the stanchions, moving with waves and whitecaps. We would never have used this playground, in spite of its convenience, if it hadn't been for its high boxed-in baby swings which Dotsie loved.

We rolled through the gate, and as soon as we came to a stop, Dotsie predictably ran to the nearest swing. Always before she had waited for me, but today, for the first time, she reached up and gave the swing a mighty push with both hands. It came back to her, its sharp metal corner catching her just above her right eyebrow. I was halfway there at a run; I could see it happening, blood spurting from her forehead as she screamed, and I pulled her to me, trying to close the wound with my hand. I hauled her up on my stomach with her face ground into my shoulder, and sprinted to the nearest emergency room nearly a half-mile away. As I ran, Dotsie stopped crying and only whimpered, perched on my stomach with her arms wrapped tightly around my neck.

The doctor in the emergency room gave her six stitches, telling me that since the cut was in her eyebrow, the scar would barely show. I had been so relieved, but now, as I lay in the hospital, I was sure that the pressure of Dotsie sitting on my stomach had somehow dislodged the placenta. I tortured myself with chastisements. If only I'd been more careful, if only I'd put her on my hip like a sensible person, if only I hadn't gone out when it was so cold, and on and on. Even when the doctor said it wasn't a factor, I persisted in believing it must have been.

If the baby did in fact have a problem, I didn't want to blame my obstetrician, who had guided me through my pregnancy with her enormous warmth, humor, and expertise. I had regarded her as a mentor, and was loath to even question her, much less find fault, or sue her for malpractice. In my family we didn't sue. If I tripped on your walkway, it was because of my own clumsiness, not your loose stone. I instinctively looked to myself as the culprit.

Ruminating about Dotsie's injury and my apparently destructive response didn't improve my mood as I lay in bed recovering from childbirth and major surgery. Until today, I had thought a cesarean section was a somewhat dangerous but interesting way to bypass labor, and I was woefully unprepared for agony which had me crying out for painkillers at all hours. The problem was the afterpains, a kind of phantom, residual labor which I hadn't even known existed. Combined with my one hundred and forty stitches, the knifelike gas pains that often accompany abdominal surgery, the Ergotrate in my IV, and my general state of angst, I was in a degree of pain I hadn't known was possible, much less bearable. My stomach would literally stand up in stiff peaks every few minutes, and nothing doctors could give me short of oblivion was enough.

When I finally felt better, and our new baby's stay in the incubator was finished, I held her for the first time. She looked like Bill and his side of the family, which made the name we'd chosen all the more suitable: Georgiana, after Bill's mother and sister. I checked her out carefully, thinking how perfectly made she was, and how impossibly tiny, with her little fists in random motion, and every finger and toe formed just right.

But there was something disturbing about her eyes. They were as blue as blueberries, just the way Dotsie's had been, but they seemed unusually unfocused, even for a newborn, and didn't search out my face the way Dotsie's had. It upset me also that she nursed eagerly but would collapse into sleep after only a minute at the most. The nurses told me to flick the soles of her feet to keep her awake, which I hated to do, but this would only net me ten more seconds of feeding before she took another little nap. She needed to nurse every few minutes, and to try to extend the interval to a reasonable length of time like an hour seemed a far-off dream.

I began to panic over how I was going to nurse Georgie every few minutes around the clock, and quailed at the thought of going home. Since I believed wholeheartedly in demand feeding, that's what I was planning to do. And I was going to take care of my husband and my two-year-old and my house, and recover from abdominal surgery, all at the same time, like any red-blooded woman.

The thought that I might be neglecting myself, and that it might backfire eventually, didn't occur to me. When I was growing up, we were what my parents laughingly referred to as *nouveau pauvre*, which meant long on lineage and short on cash. Vacation houses were lent to us, private schools were attended on scholarship, and formal clothes were purchased secondhand. We were always scrimping, borrowing, and making do. Although my husband's family's distance from the palmy days was far shorter, the coping mechanisms were similar: Keep the house going even if it's built of stilts in quicksand (rented), and hope a relative bequeaths some money and/or Dad recoups. Cheerful martyrdom was the order of the day. And if this engendered hidden agendas, and ego strength derived from dancing on sloping decks, at least the rules of the game were clear: you ate what was on your plate, and if you bit off more than you could chew, you chewed it anyway.

Georgie lost so much weight in the hospital that she was only four pounds eleven ounces on the day we went home. Bill could literally hold her in the palm of his hand. Since normal tiny baby clothes fell off her, we dressed her in clothes Dotsie contributed (with great delight) from her dolls' wardrobe.

After coming to see us and taking a look around, Bill's mother decided we needed a baby nurse, and treated us to the same woman who had bailed me out after Dotsie was born. When Miss MacMillan, whom I revered, marched in, she ordered me to wean Georgie to a bottle because she wasn't gaining weight properly on my weak, watery, insufficient milk. "She needs the richness of the formula," she said. "And she'll then be able to give you more time between feedings."

I gave way with barely a murmur, even though I wanted to continue to nurse. Sure enough, Georgie began to fill out and sleep for hours at a stretch, and I began to do the same. Miss MacMillan, in her starched white uniform and shiny white oxfords, insisted that I was attaching far too much importance to breastfeeding, and assured me that Georgie would do perfectly well on formula like most other babies, in the long as well as the short run. I consoled myself that at least she didn't try to force a four-hour schedule on us the way the medical profession had done in the years when my brothers and I were babies. We all knew what that did to you. At least Georgie got to eat when she wanted to, even if it was from a bottle.

The nurse stayed for a week, long enough to get all of us organized and rested, but after she left, my suspicion that something was wrong with Georgie continued to grow. By the time she was a month old, I was absolutely certain of it. Her eyes were still completely unfocused, and she wouldn't grab my finger, something Dotsie had done almost immediately, something babies did instinctively and automatically. Also, I couldn't get her to smile. I tried to chalk everything up to her prematurity, thinking she'd catch up, but I was afraid she was retarded, and was baffled by how she didn't seem to care whether or not she was held, fussed over, sung to, or cooed at. She acted detached, as if she lived in her own world, as content as a goldfish. I thought it was crazy, but I felt snubbed by her. I felt rejected by my own baby. And then I would tell myself, "How silly, you must be imagining things." And I would buck myself up and tell myself she'd outgrow it, trying to believe that she would suddenly become alert, responsive, and loving.

The pediatrician kept insisting she was fine, and when I took her to another pediatrician, he couldn't find anything either. Neurologically she checked out perfectly. "Just love her a lot," he said, which I took as a slur against my character, as if to say I hadn't loved her enough and that was the problem. "Maybe there's some truth in it," I chided myself, even though I knew I had learned more about love with Georgie, my second child, than I had with Dotsie, who had made me nervous because she was my first. With Georgie I felt a steady unconditional affection. But in spite of its consistency and intensity, I wanted the doctor to be right because if it was my fault, then I could change in some way and the problem might be solved.

In terms of actual cuddling and stimulation, I was finding it hard to give as much to Georgie as I had to her sister since Georgie didn't respond. So I made extra efforts to hold her and talk to her more. But still, she gave absolutely no response and no sign of the slightest improvement. It was hard to give what wasn't apparently wanted, acknowledged, or appreciated, and to deal with the alarming fact that this was a baby who preferred to be left alone. She would focus on her bottle or a toy but not on me. She wouldn't look at me or make baby noises; she ignored me completely. And although she happily held objects, she wouldn't hold my finger or grab my nose or snuggle cozily against me when I rocked her. This seemingly brilliant ability to distinguish between the animate and the inanimate completely baffled me and hurt my feelings—her rejection seemed so deliberate. Even when I saw that it applied to all living creatures, I still took it personally and was extremely upset by it, wondering whether she was picking up some kind of rejection signal from me and whether the pediatrician who had told me to love her a lot thought this.

Dotsie's godfather, one of Bill's best friends, committed suicide three weeks after Georgie was born, and my father died suddenly two weeks later. I thought maybe my grief had rebounded in some awful subconscious way on Georgie. Was that why she just lay there, maddeningly, day after day, watching her fingers twist and wave in the air? Thinking it was even remotely possible made me feel so guilty and inadequate that I couldn't bear to think about it. I was so heavily into parenthood, the Montessori method, and helping children grow up to lead fulfilling and independent lives, it was excruciating to think that I might have caused Georgie's total tune-out and stubborn, self-destructive autonomy. My confidence as a mother began to erode even though the idea that something was organically wrong with her, something she had been born with, stayed with me.

Ironically, as tension levels were escalating, and Bill and I were feeling less and less like Ozzie and Harriet, a friend of my mother's, the fashion editor of the *Daily News*, sent some photographers over to do a picture story called "Where Do All the Debs Go?" Impoverished gentry can come out on a shoestring, and I had. The deb parties I'd gone to had intimidated me, although some of them were fun. I wondered how many debutantes went straight into the diaper pail like me, and it gave me a lift to do the story, with Bill and I and our babies trying to look elegant and relaxed in a double-page spread. I could pretend to be glamorous again. We had to tickle Georgie to get her to smile for the camera but at least she looked straight at the lens. She looked perfectly normal in those pictures.

This was a bright spot in an otherwise scary landscape. I was devastated by my father's death—he was the first person I loved who had died, and I took it very hard. He was sixty-eight, and although he'd had hardening of the arteries for years, I'd felt safe and optimistic about his health since he'd given up drinking and smoking. I'd believed he'd go on for decades. His death was a complete shock, and I felt a hollow grief far more intense than any bad feeling I'd ever had. Coming on top of my worries about Georgie, my doubtful marriage, my rambunctious two-year-old, and not much sleep in the last six months, I knew I was in danger of unraveling.

As Georgie's strange, remote behavior gradually got to Bill, he joined me in feeling mystified and helpless, and somehow our fights, which had always been bad, got much worse. We were tense about so many things now, and were facing serious financial problems along with our fears for our marriage and Georgie's health. We felt overwhelmed, and didn't know where to turn.

On a cold night in January, I went off to baby-sit for a couple in our baby-sitting pool. I always liked taking care of the Wingate kids because the atmosphere in their apartment was so orderly and peaceful that it seemed to rub off on me. When Judy and her husband got home, I stayed a few minutes and she asked me how things were going. Generally reticent about my true feelings, I found myself blurting out that things were not going well. I told her I was depressed, and that my father had died recently. When I said, "I can't stand the thought that I'll never see him again," she gave me a book to read called *Life After Death*, and I found its unemotional treatment of the subject convincing and comforting. It was written by H. Ralph Harlow, a Christian intellectual who had no difficulty believing the Lord's Prayer, who believed in visions, and who accepted Christian doctrine as gospel. Since I mainly veered between agnosticism and atheism, especially lately, and hadn't believed since childhood in a personal god, and sneered at cars with JESUS SAVES on their bumpers, it was a revelation to me to find a bright, jargon-free, apolemical writer with such a straightforward belief. I decided it made sense, and told several friends that I now believed in angels, heaven, God—the whole bit. Wasn't it great? But my belief was like an air pocket in a sea of depression, and it didn't last long.

When Georgie was six months old, she formed a particular attachment to a large, empty, grooved spool of thread I gave her from my workbasket. Dotsie's play group had started a month before, and one morning she and another little girl were drawing on a sheet of newsprint as Georgie lay in her playpen. Two little boys in the group were listening to me play the guitar and sing, and another child was leaning over the side, trying to get Georgie's attention. She reached over and waved in Georgie's face. "Hi, baby! Hi, baby!" she said. Georgie, who was playing with her empty spool of thread, didn't react. She didn't even blink.

"Hi, baby. Hi, baby," the two-year-old yelled, and then yelled it again, even louder. She reached down and patted Georgie's face and got no response. She turned and looked over at Dotsie. "Your sister won't look at me. She won't play."

"She never plays with anybody," Dotsie said. God knows she had tried endlessly and I wondered how much she minded. She was deprived of a little sister/playmate just as I was deprived of a happy, gurgling, affectionate baby. Georgie never seemed to notice the attempts made to get her attention, and at this point she just kept turning her spool over and over in her little hands, intent on the wooden grooves. I put down my guitar and approached the playpen. I pried Georgie's hands away from the spool and tried to get her to grasp one of my fingers. She didn't cooperate, but kept her palm open, a seemingly deliberate action. I found myself overwhelmed with feelings of frustration and helplessness. It had happened so consistently, so many times. *Why* wouldn't she hold on to *me* instead of saving herself for inanimate objects? And why didn't she respond to Dotsie, or Bill, or other children? Or animals?

"Georgie," I said softly. But I knew by now that no matter how I said it she wouldn't react. I could croon, wheedle, coo, or yell, and nothing ever broke through her reserve. "Georgie, look at Mommy, look here!" I snapped my fingers, holding up the spool in my other hand. "Look!" Georgie just stared at her hands as she held them up over her head, waving her fingers. I picked up a rattle with colorful beads on it and shook it directly in her line of vision. "Georgie, look! See the rattle?" She ignored the rattle as well as me, focusing only on her hands. She didn't seem to like rattles and never played with them. She didn't like her bear with the music box in it either. I gave her back the spool, which she grasped, fondled, and gazed at, and I went back to my guitar playing.

I kept up a steady round of songs for a while, singing nursery rhymes to simple tunes I'd made up, and pretty soon the mothers began to arrive to pick up their kids. We were all friends, but I couldn't get through to them about Georgie, and was afraid they might think it was my fault. I was ashamed and embarrassed and didn't want to be criticized, so I passed Georgie off as normal. It was easy to do as she wasn't disruptive and, in fact, seemed to them to be incredibly good. When I tried to discuss it frankly with the mother I was closest to, asking her if she didn't think Georgie was *too* good, she said that if anything was wrong with Georgie, she would probably outgrow it.

Georgie's development schedule for gross motor activity, as they say in the books, was about two months behind what Dotsie's had been. She was nine months old when she first sat up. On day, in the spring, we went to the Pierrepont Street playground, which had a huge sandbox. As Dotsie charged around playing with her friends, Georgie sat in the sandbox for an hour and a half pouring sand through her fingers, spellbound. With a strange, stiff smile on her face, she lifted one hand high in the air and poured out the sand in a steady stream, sifting it through the fingers of her other hand over and over again. She was as oblivious of the other children as ever, and they instinctively left her alone.

That night, after supper, I picked Georgie up and she was as unresponsive as usual. My little lump, I called her. I sat down in the rocking chair, and arranged her on my lap so that she lay against me, her arms hanging limply at her sides. Dotsie was standing there with her beat-up old flannel receiving blanket in her hand, half of it trailing on the floor. She looked up at me with serious eyes.

"Here, Dotsie, climb up."

"Dotsie sit in the middle." She never got to sit in the middle.

"You can't, sweetheart, we have to wedge Georgie in so she won't fall off. How about if I rock you alone after she's asleep?" Dotsie sighed, gripping her beloved blanket, and climbed up. She leaned against her sister, sucking her thumb and nestling as best she could, as I put my arms around both of them and began to rock. Georgie drifted off to sleep as I sang, and Dotsie, at my signal, crept off my lap and stood waiting. I put Georgie in her crib and went over to Dotsie, swinging her up into my arms. What a comfort she was. She clutched me around my neck and snuggled against me.

"Sing horsies, Mommy," she whispered, already half asleep. "All the Pretty Little Horses" was our favorite lullaby, and she was out cold by the time I got to the end.

Because Georgie woke up so much in the night, Bill and I had long since relinquished our bedroom to her so she wouldn't wake Dotsie. We slept on the convertible sofa in the living room. The prevailing theory of the time admonished us not to give in to the baby—"Show him who's in charge, and if he's comfortable, dry, and fed, firmly put him down and let him cry if he wants to. He'll soon get the idea that it's bedtime." We had never let Georgie cry before, believing that the rigid four-hour schedules we'd been on as babies could turn you into a Machiavellian compulsive personality with a starvation complex. But that night, exhausted and confused, we decided we would see if she would cry herself back to sleep when she woke up in the night. We figured the fresh air in the sandbox must have tired her out. At three in the morning she woke up and cried pitifully, but we steeled ourselves, sitting close to each other on the edge of the bed, hoping and praying that she'd stop. Soon the telephone rang. Georgie's crying had disturbed our next door neighbor and she called to complain and take issue with us.

"You mustn't let the baby cry like that," she said angrily. "You've got to pick her up and comfort her, it's terrible to let a baby cry." And she slammed down the receiver. Feeling as if we'd been accused of child abuse, I said, "Well, there goes *that* theory." I picked Georgie up with a mixture of relief and resignation and rocked her while Bill fixed a bottle. She didn't sleep through the night once until she was two, but at least she would settle right down once she got her bottle. For me it was a different story, and once awakened, I often couldn't get back to sleep again.

Georgie started to walk at fourteen months and from the beginning she seemed to be supercareful. She never pulled lamps over or broke a vase, and if she was destructive, it was on purpose. She couldn't stand the phonograph, for instance. One day, in the middle of Burl Ives singing "The Little White Duck," she went over, hefted the phonograph, and would have sent it crashing to the floor if I hadn't been there. I set it on a table out of reach and put the record back on, and Georgie went over to the far side of the room and rocked on all fours. She had started doing this from the time she could crawl and it drove us nuts. She could stay with it for hours. When she rocked her crib all the way across the floor, we attached it to the wall with hook eyes and wire. Sometimes she banged her head gently on the crib or the wall, not really hurting herself but keeping up an eerie rhythm with a little archaic smile on her face. If I tried to stop her, she would always go back to it.

Right after she started walking, she came over to me while I was playing the guitar, grabbed it, and threw it on the floor. I yelled at her and she, with her consistent and total lack of affect, just ambled away and went over to rock against the wall. I'm sure she didn't feel remorse or fear at being reprimanded. The only feelings in her emotional vocabulary seemed to be fascination, indifference, and hunger. When I played another song, she came over and yanked the guitar again. No discipline of any kind ever made the slightest impression on Georgie. She was going to do what she was going to do. I felt utterly useless in the face of it, and found alarming concepts like "changeling" and "bad seed" occurring to me. That she was "mad" was also a possibility, even more horrifying than the others. But I was consoled by the fact that she never actually hurt anyone, including the cat, whose favorite spot for a nap was curled up against Georgie when she was asleep. When Georgie would wake up and find the cat snuggled against her, she was indifferent. Her avoidance of contact included all living creatures without exception.

One of the harmless things she enjoyed was playing at the bathroom sink. She stood there for hours, letting the water cascade through her fingers in a small, steady stream. She never touched the faucets or made a mess. Her eyes, huge and hypnotic, with a thick fringe of dark lashes, stared at the water as if it was totally entertaining.

Georgie was almost a year and a half old when Dotsie, who was three, started going to nursery school and having problems. Dotsie had been fine in play group so it came as a big shock when her teacher complained that she was aggressive, "said bad words," and fell apart easily. I was very upset. Dotsie's teacher wanted to know if her problems in school could be related to tension in the home. She suggested Bill and I go for counseling. We knew we should but couldn't afford it. I began to dread picking Dotsie up at school every day for fear of what they were going to tell me. At this point I was blaming just about everything on "tension in the home." Bill had begun stopping off at the Blarney Rose to fortify himself on his way home from the office. And I began to lose my temper more often, getting mad, primarily, at Dotsie and Bill. I didn't get angry at Georgie because she was too vulnerable and, frankly, too unresponsive. It was clear to me that she couldn't help whatever was going on with her, and I felt as helpless in the face of it as she must have.

I started having depressions that would immobilize me for two or three hours sometimes on the weekends when Bill was home and I could collapse. I would just sit, feeling like a concrete block trying to fly, as my mother would say. Another of her favorite expressions was that it was wrong to live beyond your emotional income, and I felt I was doing that in spades these days. Sometimes at night I would rail at Bill and cry, telling him that everything would be fine if we just had a decent-sized apartment and more money. So we moved to a larger apartment, a big old garden duplex a few blocks away, and both of us began making more money because I got another book assignment from Scholastic and he changed jobs. But nothing helped.

One morning, after a particularly violent episode the night before, I began to think we ought to separate. But fundamentally I didn't believe in divorce and felt that the worst of our fighting was my own fault for provoking him. At this point I knew that counseling would have helped because I had begun to be afraid of Bill and I wasn't sure I could trust him. But somehow we kept thinking we could figure it all out on our own. Bill's mild and gentlemanly facade, contrasting with my feisty, outgoing personality, helped persuade our families that the solution lay in my finding a way to "improve my disposition." I was supposed to shape up and get happy.

After we moved, Bill started buying a quart of cheap sherry every night on his way home and drinking all of it in the course of the evening. Once I bought him a gallon, and he was annoyed. "I can limit myself to a quart a night if that's all I have in the house," he said. I didn't join him in his drinking unless we were going to a party, and I didn't realize he was developing a problem. When he would get quietly ossified in front of the television after I went to bed, I felt neglected, but I thought it was probably because he was unhappy with me. After all, he hadn't indulged this way before we were married.

I began to feel as if Bill and I were in a flooding room. Although the water was inexorably rising, he was still tall enough to keep his head above the water but I was submerged. If we were to survive, someone was going to have to open the door and let the water out, and it would be either Bill, or me, or someone on the other side.

Working on the book and ferreting out maxims helped me keep my mind off my troubles. A friend of mine and I worked out a regular baby-sitting swap whereby her son and Georgie could keep each other company in order to give me the time I needed in the library. It was not a great success. The children only played side by side—parallel play, it was called. The little boy was annoyed that he could never get Georgie to join in an activity.

On the two mornings I stayed home, Georgie and I often cooked together, baking or making a casserole. It became a hobby we could share. Bill and I were in a quasivegetarian, health food phase, had given up meat, and like to have cheese soufflé once a week. Georgie particularly enjoyed making soufflés, and I thought my interest in them must have been contagious. She would climb up on the step stool by the stove and watch the butter melting in the pan, and then she would help me stir the sauce, handling the spoon with great dexterity. She would stare into the pot as if the textures and colors had unusual appeal for her. When we were cooking, I would often try to get her to talk.

"Georgie, say *cook*," I would say. "Georgie's cooking. Say *cook*." But she would answer me only with steady, intent stirring. "We'll eat when Daddy gets home. Can you say *Daddy*? Da-dee." She seemed so intelligently deliberate in her refusal to look at me or repeat my words. "Can you say *eat*? EAT." I would put my fingers in my mouth and make munching noises but there was never a response. I felt helpless and frustrated as well as mystified, and only hoped that she'd talk when she was ready. After all, she wasn't even two yet. Meanwhile, she certainly had her strengths. In addition to her mixing and stirring capabilities, she never dropped things, and could have complete charge of the glass measuring cup. She never fell down or hurt herself either, always maintaining her stance on the step stool without wavering. She seemed to have a phenomenal sense of balance, and I wondered if she'd inherited her father's ability as a dancer.

She was always completely absorbed in cooking and baking until I got out the electric beater. Then she would climb down and start to leave the kitchen. When I turned it on, she would retreat to the far side of the living room, where she would get down on her hands and knees and begin to rock, back and forth, staring straight ahead. When I turned off the beater, she would stop her rocking and come back into the kitchen. I didn't know what caused her reaction, whether she was afraid of catching a finger or whether the noise bothered her. But her reaction was consistent.

When it was clean-up time and I took my pans and bowls to the sink to wash, again she would walk quietly away. If I asked her to help me with the dishes, she ignored me. Why, when she loved to play in the bathroom sink with the water running, wouldn't she like helping me with the dishes? It was a mystery. She must be contrary, I thought, like Mary Mary in the nursery rhyme.

Chapter 2

Anguish

Our new apartment was really half of a very old house. It was going to be a while, if ever, before we got it in shape, but we had managed to paint the living room yellow and white, and we could sit there and read the Sunday *Times* after church and enjoy ourselves. Church was, as usual, a nice break, a chance to relax in a peaceful atmosphere with grown-ups while Dotsie enjoyed herself in Sunday school and Georgie went to the nursery. I prayed fervently, as always, for strength to get through the next week. I didn't have a strong faith, and except for Sunday mornings and an occasional flash, I felt that depending on God was an insult to my self-reliance. And surely He had better things to do than worry about me. Lately, though, I had taken to playing all my records of Handel's *Messiah* on weekday afternoons, curling up on the sofa while Georgie amused herself nearby. It seemed to have the effect of expanding my spiritual consciousness.

Maybe because there were never any complaints about the children in Sunday school, we were always in a good mood after church, and looked forward to reading the paper. Following our usual routine, Bill picked up the business section and I chose the magazine section, and as I glanced through it, an article called "Where Self

Begins" by Bruno Bettelheim caught my eye. One sentence in particular alarmed me. "Our studies concentrate on autistic children—youngsters who have totally shut themselves off from all relations with others." I read the rest of the article with a feeling of growing dread. I had never heard of autism or Bettelheim but learned that he was an authority who had worked in the field for twenty years, and that autism was a disorder characterized by withdrawn behavior, rocking, head banging, finger twirling, poor eye contact, and often, aphasia, or the inability to talk. Georgie fit right in.

The article was based on the behavior of children in Bettelheim's Orthogenic School in Chicago. The fact that these children were in an institution made it possible for me to block some of my feelings of recognition. After all, Georgie wasn't and surely never would be in such a place. She wasn't that bad! But my heart sank as I read on, trying to absorb Bettelheim's conviction that autism was caused by mothers who either ignored or overpowered their babies.

"What explains the near-total arrest in personality development in some human beings?" Whatever it was, he wrote as if he knew the answer. "The most important thing we have learned is this: personality depends on the child's own spontaneous reaction to the conditions of his life." In other words, it doesn't begin to develop until the child is *born*. "Our work demonstrates how important it is that from birth on the child gets responses from the environment that encourage his spontaneous moves toward the world; he should not be ignored or overpowered." Then he warns, "Things may go terribly wrong if the world is experienced as basically frustrating too soon." He then pronounced that "The decisive factor . . . is whether or not the infant is encouraged to act on his own to reach a goal—and how much so."

I put down the paper, feeling as if the world had suddenly turned gray. Although my suspicion that Georgie was brain damaged couldn't be shaken, still, was it possible that I had exacerbated existing tendencies in some way? Surely I hadn't been the actual *cause* of them, had I? The fact that someone as well educated and highly regarded as Bettelheim thought so was the most profoundly unsettling news I'd ever had. I felt as though I were being accused of a crime I didn't even know I'd committed. I would have to answer to society as well as myself, my husband, Dotsie, Georgie, and my extended family. And yet it didn't make sense, because I'd tried so hard with Georgie, and couldn't get her to relate to me or anyone else no matter what I did.

By the time I'd finished reading the article, Bill had gone into the kitchen to get some coffee. I didn't share my feelings with him. It was easier to crawl back into denial, to insist to myself that Georgie wasn't really autistic, just a little slow in some ways, maybe because she'd been premature. And overshadowed by her rambunctious older sister, that was it. And she took after her father, who was extremely quiet.

However, Bettelheim wrote with such authority that I found it hard to believe he could be wrong. Although my own experience told me he couldn't be right either, I didn't have the self-confidence to fight him, partly because I was burned out by being the mother of a child like Georgie, loving someone all day every day who evidently couldn't love me.

To cap things, two weeks later I came across a short critique of Bettelheim's book *The Empty Fortress* in the back of the New York *Times Book Review*: "Foremost among the handful of psychiatrists and psychologists who have dedicated themselves to unraveling the puzzle of autistic behavior is Bruno Bettelheim. No brief review can do justice to his wisdom and compassion. At first glance, Dr. Bettelheim's theory of autism seems disarmingly simple: he suggests that autistic behavior results from an infant's conviction that it has no effect upon its environment. The mothers of such infants fail to react appropriately to their baby's needs. Perhaps they feed the child when it wishes to be entertained, or misconstrue a conflict in the feeding situation as a rejection of them, and then react with hatred toward the baby. Sometimes the effect upon the child is profound enough to cause autism; occasionally it is severe enough to cause death."

This time I discussed all of it with Bill and he reassured me.

"Well, I know one thing and that is you don't hate Georgie. She's not like those kids that much anyway. He says autistic children act like wild animals, rock all the time, and hurt themselves. Georgie's not like that."

"You mean because she only rocks *sometimes*. And because she doesn't hurt herself when she bangs her head against the crib? But I'm worried about how withdrawn she is."

"She's going to talk, don't worry. And then she'll never stop, just like her sister. I didn't talk much when I was her age. She'll be okay. Anyway, this guy is a psychologist and those people are all screwed up. He probably hates his own mother."

I was happy to try to believe him.

Toward the end of February, the same month the articles appeared, Dotsie celebrated her fourth birthday with exactly four little friends and I discovered the Brooklyn Heights of Folly, a local talent show. The rehearsals got me out of the house, and gave me an opportunity to meet new people, and the show itself was fun as well. The director and writer, Lee Kneerim, was a gifted local luminary, and Jim Sellars, a composer who lived in the neighborhood, supplied an appealing original score. A collection of local talent gave of their time, energy, and considerable professionalism. Since accents were my specialty, the director wrote a skit for me in which I played six people of varying nationalities, flitting behind a screen for each change of accessories. On stage I had always played everything for laughs, and was sure that when my children were older, if my dreams could come true, I would be a comedienne like Phyllis Diller or Carol Burnett. Meanwhile, at least I could have five nights of fun doing a funny skit playing six people in fifteen minutes, and standing on my head (literally) to sing a solo.

After the show our pediatrician said, "Why don't you cheer everybody up at home doing your accents? I had no idea you were so funny." I took it to mean that she thought the atmosphere at my house was depressing, and that it was my fault. I didn't have a comeback for her. I was not at a point where I could explain that I could stand on my head and sing "Puff the Magic Dragon" with smoke coming out of my ears and Georgie wouldn't even look up, much less acknowledge it.

My feelings of inadequacy as a mother were multiplied when I read Eliot Fremont-Smith's featured review of *The Empty Fortress* in the New York *Times*. "Autistic children are those who, for no known organic reason, have failed to develop a personality, an ego-sense that can operate in relation to real experience." It described the condition as "one of the severest forms of childhood schizophrenia . . . an illness, even a suicide, of the soul."

The review went on to state that autistic infants *choose* to be autistic. "Of course one cannot speak of infants 'making choices,' yet some kind of choice, no less real for being prelogical, seems apparent in the autistic child's rigid and complexly defended withdrawal from effective relations with other people and the world." Bettelheim said that whenever he and his staff were able to penetrate an autistic child's defenses, they found "hatred, extreme and explosive. And behind that hatred was always the longing, eternally thwarted, but nevertheless not given up; a longing now deeply encapsulated in repression so as to keep it from coming to awareness in unbearable pain." I quote to avoid being accused of exaggeration. ". . . the hatred and longing stem from extreme frustrations in the mother-infant relationship which result in the infant's conviction that it can have no effect upon its environment. This conviction . . . is, must be, absolutely shattering, for only through repeated and satisfying experiences of its effect upon its surroundings, starting from birth, can an infant develop a personality, a sense of 'I.' "

After reading this, Bill and I told ourselves that Georgie wasn't that bad, and that surely she would outgrow it. We couldn't see that I was guilty as accused. Granted, I had been tired out and distracted since Georgie was born, but wasn't that normal for a mother with a busy two-year-old and an alarmingly unresponsive baby? I had thought I was committed to helping our children become independent in every way possible, and encouraging them in the broadest possible range of expression and choice. But Bettelheim was accusing me of a vast hidden agenda, a kind of passive infanticide.

Several months later I saw an episode of "Marcus Welby, M.D." about an autistic child who was sent to live in a special school when he was four because that was the only way he was going to get better. The boy and his mother were duplicates of Georgie and me. I couldn't face it because the thought of Georgie living anywhere but at home was totally unacceptable, as unthinkable as walking in front of a bus.

The Follies went off as scheduled in the spring, and right after the show was over, Georgie celebrated her second birthday. There was no point in inviting anybody as it wouldn't make any difference to her, so we had a family party. When I brought in her cake with candles, she could not, or would not, blow them out. We demonstrated, wheedled, and pleaded but nothing would induce her to make the least effort even though she became totally involved with the frosting. I couldn't figure out how she could help me make a soufflé and yet couldn't blow out her own candles.

Soon after the cake episode, when I was despairing of her ever taking any direction, Georgie brought me her sneakers while I was sitting in the garden. She stood there looking at them and then took them from me, sat down, and tried to put them on. I helped her out, and then I had an idea. Dotsie still couldn't tie her shoes but I had a hunch about Georgie.

"Let's learn how to tie your shoes, Georgie." She sat on some flagstones in front of me and concentrated on the laces, the trees making a play of light around her. "Over and under, make a loop, that's right." She worked hard, repeating the process. Around went the shoelace for the final turn, the second loop emerged, she pulled the laces tight and Georgie had tied her shoe. No two-year-old I knew could do that, and the child behavior books said it wouldn't happen until much later. We did it a few more times until she really had it down, and then she put on her other sneaker, tied it with a little help, and walked away. No glance in my direction or shy smile of victory. She didn't seem to feel a sense of accomplishment, but she tied her shoes faithfully from then on. Soon after that my mother-in-law said, "I don't know what could be wrong with Georgie because she's certainly not a *stupid* child."

"Maybe *I'm* the one who needs help," I ventured. "Maybe I should see a psychiatrist."

"Oh good heavens," she said. "What do they know? I'm sure they couldn't tell you anything I couldn't tell you. There's nothing wrong with you anyway. Why can't you be like Mrs. Smith's daughter? She has six children, brings them up herself, and never complains."

Soon after Georgie's feat of dexterity with her sneakers, she began to draw. Dotsie was our artist-in-residence, and one morning in June, when school was out for the summer, she assembled her materials and lay on her stomach on the floor drawing pictures. I had read a book about how to foster creativity in your children that advised keeping an unlimited supply of paper, markers, and pens on hand and allowing free access to the materials. In order to avoid stifling the creative process, the author also advised saying "How interesting!" rather than "How great!" when presented with a masterpiece. I adopted this as my standard reaction, and kept a ream of typing paper and a bunch of pens and markers on a low shelf.

When Georgie decided it was time to begin her career as an artist, she carefully took a piece of paper off the top and got down on all fours across from her sister. She began by swirling curlecues, and stayed within the confines of the paper, mercifully uninterested in creating on her clothes or the walls. She kept drawing long after Dotsie got tired of it and went out to play.

We were expecting a hot summer, and my mother-in-law treated us to a monthlong stay in a charming, airy cottage on an island. We wanted to stay there forever. We took along a mother's helper so we could have a real vacation, and she was patient with the kids and a delight to have around. She seemed to take it in stride that Georgie kept to herself and didn't relate to anyone. "At least she's

easy," she said. All we had to do on rainy days was supply Georgie
with paper and markers, and on the good days she was always happy
to be at the beach on the Sound. She would play in the little wavelets,
looking down at the water for hours, watching it break into shining
fragments and pinpoints of light over her fingers and toes. She would
squat down and scrutinize patterns in the sand, symmetrical ripples
left by the waves, and she'd stroke the smooth insides of shells, and
look at their colors and grooves as if she saw things we didn't see
and was fascinated by them.

One day, when it was overcast and too gray for the beach,
Dotsie and Georgie were playing outside while I sat under a tree
contentedly reading. I looked up to find that Georgie had gone off
to take a snooze under a bush. She had done the same thing the
summer before this, and now here she was again, out cold and curled
up like a puppy. She seemed to like the coolness of the dirt in the
shade and the coziness of the small space. No wonder Bill had started
calling her "George Dog." That term of endearment always bothered
me because she was like a pet in many ways. In addition to sleeping
under bushes, she was easily amused, basically only interested in
food and sleep, and she didn't talk. But unlike a pet, or a dog anyway,
she wouldn't look at you and seemed to have no loyalty. Anyone
could feed her, take care of her, hold her, put her to bed, get her
up—she didn't seem to discriminate at all among caretakers. She
had never cried when I went out and had never been glad to see
me. Increasingly I blamed myself, thinking I must have failed her
in some way, that she suffered from a kind of emotional failure to
thrive. I had the feeling that Bill was beginning to have some doubts
about me as well, although he never said so. Since he'd always
thought I was too cerebral, maybe he thought I'd been cold with
Georgie. He agreed with his mother when she told me that she
thought I was an intellectual, and it was definitely not a compliment.
The way she used to say it—"intellectewal"—made me cringe, and
to have it a pejorative term was incomprehensible to me as intellec-
tuality had been given the highest value in my family when I was
growing up.

When we got home from our wonderful month, Dotsie, at four, went into her second year of nursery school. She had made it through her first year and I was working with her on her behavior. I had thought it would be helpful if she dramatized her life in pictures—her problems, pleasures, likes and dislikes—and we had worked together faithfully with this. The art therapy got us communicating in a closer way and seemed to have calmed her down.

I geared up for Georgie's terrible twos but they never arrived. Georgie didn't become demanding, insistent, or willful—she just quietly existed in her own world, amusing herself and relating to no one. Bugs were the only creatures she would have anything to do with. And no amount of cajoling, manipulating, or entreating on my part would get her to say anything. She said "goggy" once when I held out a cookie but I could never get her to say it again, whether I withheld the cookie or not.

I decided I would have to muster the courage to take *The Empty Fortress* out of the library. I didn't know enough about autism, and it was time. When I brought the book home, I put it on the dining room table and left it there as if it were radioactive. I was afraid to pick it up, as if to do so would ensure my indictment for mysterious, unintentional, unforgivable crimes.

One afternoon, when Georgie was playing quietly with inter-locking plastic blocks (she never played with dolls or stuffed animals) and Dotsie was still in school, I thought I'd delve into the book for an hour or so, biting the bullet like a big girl. I flipped it open and read, at random, "Autism is a defense against unbearable anxiety . . . the source of this anxiety is not an organic impairment but the child's evaluation of the conditions of his life as being utterly de-structive." I couldn't read any further. I put the book down, shut it decisively, and returned it to the library that same afternoon. I was ambivalent—I knew Bettelheim was wrong but . . . what if? And who was I to doubt a respected authority like him? Maybe I just couldn't face myself.

Just what *did* I feel so guilty about? What was it about my behavior when Georgie was a baby that I thought could possibly

have caused autism? First of all, I was trying to come to terms with
the fact that I was not happy with Bill, and worried that the atmosphere was tainted by our misery. He was closed and quiet,
reticent when it came to praise and affection; I was scrappy and
bossy—not a productive combination. I had told him I would have
to divorce him one day on the grounds of cruelty and neglect.
Kiddingly, I suggested several times that I would pay him fifty cents
a month for one compliment. I would get my money out and demand
my compliment but he could never think of one. Neither one of us
seemed to have much self-esteem, and this was reinforced by the
fact that his family thought we were both failures. Bill hadn't made
enough money, and I wasn't chic enough and didn't try to hide my
intelligence like a sensible female.

Part of the problem stemmed from the fact that Bill was unhappy in his choice of a career, and had allowed himself to be
railroaded into the business world by his well-meaning but unrealistic father. Bill was artistic and talented (a sissy in his Dad's eyes);
he loved to paint, and was always haunting the galleries on Madison
Avenue as well as taking studio art courses. I had considered him
a romantic figure when I had first known him, gifted and misun-
derstood, and had longed to rescue him from his limiting bourgeois
background. I pictured us in a loft in SoHo, with him painting and
me walking in the door with groceries, tired from working to support
us, but happy and looking forward to eventually devoting myself
to my own artistic pursuits. Instead, he was in the brokerage business, poured into pin stripes, trying to put his heart into making
money, and I kept producing children he wasn't ready to support
emotionally or financially. Since he hadn't been much of a drinker
before we were married, I thought this and my behavior had driven
him to drink.

After we were married, it was depressing to have to jettison all
the frills in an effort to pay the bills. I could believe it when I read
that 90 percent of all marriages broke up because of money problems.
I was sure that if I hadn't gotten pregnant so easily and quickly,
not once but twice, Bill might have been able to fulfill himself. After

a while I lost sight of the fact that he'd opted for Wall Street before children and our marriage were even considered.

The fact was that Bettelheim could only get to me because I thought he might be right. I was sure I had taken advantage of the fact that Georgie was such a "good" baby and could entertain herself so easily, and I had left her too much to her own devices. And since Dotsie had been such an active, talkative, demanding, and affectionate two-year-old, she had gotten most of the attention: "The wheel that squeaks the loudest gets the grease."

On certain levels I was definitely entertaining the possibility that I had—albeit unwittingly—set the stage for Georgie's failure to develop normally. How horrendous that I could be so destructive, I thought, like a mad emotional bomber. Could it be that I had within me such awesome power as to be able to create a condition as dire as autism? Surely I should be taken out and shot, even if I hadn't done it on purpose. At the very least I should be pilloried. What was I, a kind of maternal witch? We even had a cat, and she was black.

Not long after *The Empty Fortress* episode, I lined up a friend in the baby-sitting pool who would take Georgie on a regular basis so I could finish my book. On a Monday morning, I left Georgie off and went to the library, and when I returned later on, we went into the kitchen to chat. Keeping my coat on, I sat down at the table with her.

"I have to talk to you about Georgie," she said with a grim look on her face. "I'm not going to beat around the bush about it. I have to tell you that I think you baby Georgie too much. I think you're keeping her a baby." I huddled deeper into my coat, thinking about Bettelheim and wondering if she'd read about his theories too. I felt as if the kitchen, with its white overhead light, had suddenly become an interrogation room.

"What do you mean, keeping her a baby?"

"Well, for one thing you should just take away her bottle. She doesn't need it anymore. And you should make her ask for things. You just give her anything she wants, you anticipate what she needs, and that way you're enabling her to stay immature. Make her tell you what she wants, don't give it to her unless she says the word." I felt tears welling up, and Georgie, whom I had been clutching for comfort on my lap, wriggled free and got down.

"Do *you* get her to say anything that way?" I asked.

"Well no, but that has to start at home. You teach her, and then she'll do it with other people."

"Do you think there's something wrong with her?"

"You've just got to let her grow up."

I left as fast as I could, and tried all the harder to get words out of Georgie, but she wouldn't cooperate.

Not long afterward, a similar situation occurred in the supermarket. Blitzed as usual by the variety in the cereal section, I'd been scanning it for what seemed like hours trying to find Cheerios when another mother pulled up alongside me. Like me, she had a toddler in the front of her cart and another child roaming around in the vicinity. I recognized her as one of the mothers from Dotsie's nursery school although her son was a class ahead. "How's Dotsie doing this year?" she asked.

"Well, I think things are better than last year."

"How's your other little girl?" She looked over at Georgie, who was fazing out with her fingers twirling in the air over her head.

"Oh, she's fine," I said.

"Is she talking yet?"

"No, she isn't really."

"And how old is she?"

"She's two." I always wanted to pass her off as younger.

"Well, I always say, there's nothing a human being can do that's worse than getting in the way of another's growth." With that she gave me a serious well-meaning look, smiled tentatively, and left the cereal aisle. I stood there stunned. I felt as if I'd been kicked in the stomach. I had no way of defending myself since I was beginning to think she was right. I was blocking Georgie's growth. But how? And what could I do? I couldn't seem to reach her no matter what I did. I couldn't even get her to look at me. If I were blocking her growth, it must be some murky, subconscious number I was doing on her. I forced myself back to the cereal search, and when I found the Cheerios, Georgie tried to grab the box. She wanted a handful. I held it out of reach.

"Say *Cheerios*." She gazed off into space, shutting off. "Say *Cheerios*," I hissed at her. "*Say it!*" I started to cry, threw the box in the cart, grabbed Dotsie's hand, and made for the nearest checkout line. I stood there trying to control myself and barely made it home before the floodgates opened and I headed for my pillow. Over and over again, I cried, "What am I going to do? What am I going to do?" Dotsie came over and put her hand on the back of my head.

"Don't cry, Mommy," she said. "Everything be all right."

Dotsie and Georgie got great tans in August when we were at our island house. They had new red and white bathing suits that summer, a present from Bill's mother, and they looked wonderfully healthy except for one anomaly: Dotsie's face didn't get brown.

In September, when she went back to school, she seemed tired, and after a few weeks she began complaining of a pain in her elbow. I took her to Dr. Weeks, our pediatrician, who had taken care of the children since Georgie was born. She was a tall, imposing woman in her sixties and she scared the daylights out of me. The fact that she was the sister of President Kennedy's back doctor added to her mystique. She had no trouble building a powerful practice in spite of the fact that she was critical, opinionated, and kept everyone waiting for at least an hour no matter how sick your kids were. But she was the best doctor around and made house calls, so I stuck with her.

Dr. Weeks's home and office were in her brownstone on Willow Street, three blocks from where we lived. I put Georgie in the stroller and we walked over, enjoying being outdoors as we always did, even though the stiff breeze off the harbor was a harbinger of cold blasts soon to come. Half a mile away, across the water, I could see the glistening tops of Wall Street skyscrapers. They stuck up over the railing of the promenade looking incongruous, like dominoes. The October sun warmed us as we walked along, Dotsie kicking the crackling leaves on the sidewalk as she went, and Georgie clutching her bright plastic beads. Georgie looked up periodically, her face tense and her eyes squinted into crescents. She seemed to let everything she saw wash over her as if it were too much to take in.

The waiting room was the usual welter of toys and small children, and we found a seat on a daybed and settled down for the wait. Georgie went to a corner and sat on the floor near some blocks, piling one expertly on top of the other until she had an impressive tower. Dotsie curled up beside me, nursing her sore elbow.

When it was time to see the doctor, I gathered Georgie up and took her with us into the examining room. Dr. Weeks carefully looked at Dotsie's elbow, bending her arm back and forth, and asked, "Does it hurt all the time, or just sometimes, Dotsie?"

"It aches. All the time."

"Do you remember falling on it, or hurting it in some way?"

"No," Dotsie said.

"How long has it been aching? A long time?" Dr. Weeks looked at me.

"About a week, I think," I said.

"A long time," said Dotsie. Dr. Weeks's strong face had a look of concern.

"I think we'll wait and see if it gets better, but then if it doesn't, we'll have to have it x-rayed. Is there anything else I ought to know about?"

"Well," I said, never dreaming, really, that there was the slightest connection. "She didn't get a tan on her face this summer. It was the strangest thing. Doesn't she look pale?" Dr. Weeks nodded. Dotsie had always had rosy cheeks and had seemed sturdy and robust, but now she was ashen. "And she gets so tired. The day in school, nine to three this year, seems like a lot for her. She's exhausted when she gets home. She just collapses in front of the television."

"It is a long day, and that may be all it is. Let's give this a week or so, and see what happens."

By the next week the pain was still there, so we had it x-rayed, and the x-ray showed nothing. Dr. Weeks said we would just wait and see if it got any worse. We found ourselves going to the playground less and less as the days grew colder and shorter. We began to get ready for Christmas, and although Dotsie's pain was still there, she had gotten used to it and didn't complain about it much.

Christmas engendered its usual madness and joy, and this year we all got the flu. The whole family was in a shambles, and Bill and I took turns getting out of bed to take care of one child or another. Everyone had a fever for a week and we all just had to lie there until it passed. Georgie was the first to bounce back, then Bill, and then me, and by New Year's only Dotsie was still sick. The infection had traveled to her eye and hung on for an abnormally long time. I had bundled the children up and had taken them to Dr. Weeks earlier in the week, and she had prescribed antibiotic drops for Dotsie's eye, but when the infection wouldn't clear up, I called Dr. Weeks again and she made a house call. When she arrived that night, she looked tired, apprehensive, and resigned as she trudged up the stairs and examined Dotsie in her bedroom. In addition to all the usual flu symptoms and the eye infection, Dotsie now had a pain in her knee as well as her elbow. Dr. Weeks leaned over her bed and probed gently, listening to her chest, checking her throat and her eye, and looking carefully at her knee and elbow and some bruises on her legs. She stood up wearily and gazed at me with such concern that my heart skipped a beat. She motioned me out of the room and stooped toward me as she whispered, so that Dotsie wouldn't hear, "I'm afraid we'll have to put her in the hospital." The light was dim in the hall, and the entire apartment had a feeling of darkness about it.

"In the hospital? What for?"

"I'm going to have some blood tests run on her. I'll call from here if I may. She should be admitted tonight." She used the telephone in our bedroom to call Brooklyn-Cumberland Hospital and make all the necessary arrangements. She left quickly, brushing past me on her way to the stairs. "I'll see myself out and I'll see you tomorrow at the hospital. They're expecting you, you can go right over."

Bill and I stood there in stunned silence. Dr. Weeks had seemed almost covert somehow, but we didn't have time to dwell on it. I packed up a few of Dotsie's things, and carried her out to the car wrapped in a wool blanket with a scarf around her head. Within an hour she was settled in a nice room and was sound asleep. I wanted to stay with her but was told it was against the rules, so I went home to Bill and Georgie and what sleep I could get.

The next day the doctor called to say that the hematologist at Brooklyn Hospital wanted to talk to us when we went to see Dotsie. It was a Saturday morning. We left Georgie with a sitter and fifteen minutes later Brooklyn Hospital loomed up before us looking old and dismal with its dark red brick and stalwart doors. We rode up in the elevator in silence, not daring to speculate. The doors slid open to let us out into a wide corridor with freshly waxed linoleum and enameled walls. Dr. Kaufman came to the door of her office herself and looked at us solicitously.

"Are you the hematologist?" I asked.

"Yes, I'm Dr. Kaufman. Come in." She was about fifty and had a practical air about her, all business, in her long white lab coat and laced-up black oxfords. "Please sit down." She motioned me to a chair. The office was small and impersonal, no photographs, only a gray steel desk and a few chrome and black chairs. She and I sat while Bill stood against the wall by the door. She turned to face us. "I'm afraid I have very bad news. Your daughter has leukemia."

I took a fast, deep breath, Bill moved to the back of my chair and grasped my shoulders, and the room was suddenly whiter and colder. Tears poured down my cheeks and I felt as if I were suffocating.

"How can you be sure?" Bill asked. His voice sounded hollow, and his face had a blanched look.

"I'm afraid the tests are conclusive. Of course you can get a second opinion, in fact you should get a second opinion. But I'm afraid there is no doubt that she has leukemia." Through the haze of shock and tears I noticed she had a hypodermic needle on a tray on her desk, the only medical paraphernalia in the room.

"How long has she got to live?" Bill asked.

"A year at the most." I broke down and sobbed. Dr. Kaufman lowered her voice. "Shall I give your wife a sedative?" Bill nodded and helped me off with my coat. I rolled up my sleeve like a robot and didn't even feel the jab of the needle. What I was feeling was a sense of implosion, as if a tiny nuclear bomb had gone off in my chest, and had turned me to ashes inside. My heart had splintered into shards. The pain was so brutal that no amount of medication could begin to insulate me. Bill put his arm around my shoulders, helped me get up out of the chair, and escorted me carefully down the corridor to the elevator. I couldn't stop crying and shaking. I felt as if his arm, tight around my shoulders, literally kept me from shattering. The elevator came and the packed group inside moved back quietly to make room for us. Wedged in, I cried silently as we went from floor to floor, hardly noticing the people getting on and off. As we got to the lobby, I glanced at the elevator operator. He was tall and thin and wore a shiny, stained and threadbare blue uniform, with a captain's hat on his head. "You shouldn't allow yourself to get so upset, lady," he said, and I felt as if I'd been slapped.

Fifteen minutes later we were home trying to act normal for Georgie. She was lying on the living room floor drawing pictures and she didn't look up when we came home. Thin January sunlight angled in through the windows, catching the fading sunstreaks in her hair as she drew her endless squiggles on the paper. I sat down on the floor beside her and tried to get her attention. "Dotsie's going to be in the hospital for a while, Georgie. She is very, very sick." But Georgie made no move. I got up and said hello to the baby-sitter, and after one look at our stricken faces, she didn't dare ask what was wrong. She told us Georgie had been so good she'd gotten a lot of reading done. She left quickly and I went over to Bill and cried in his arms, wishing he would cry too. Georgie just lay in her patch of sunlight, never missing a stroke with the marker, adding circles and more circles to the intricacy of her design.

As soon as I had collected myself, I went back to the hospital to see Dotsie. "Hi, Mommy." It was all I could do not to cry. I hugged her, careful of the IV attached to her arm, and kissed her cheek, which still felt hot although not as hot as yesterday. Yesterday seemed like months ago, and I would have given anything to get back there.

"I brought *Tom Kitten*," I said. It was her favorite book. She listened quietly as I read of the terrible trouble Tom was always getting into. As I was reading, a little boy wandered in and leaned against the wall, listening. He had been badly burned, the puckered scars looking stretched and painful on his neck. He stood still, lounging and listening, until I'd finished the story.

"What's your name?" I asked.

"Michael," he said.

"How old are you?"

"Four."

"Dotsie's four too, only she'll be five soon. This is Dotsie."

Dotsie smiled at him and he said, "Hi."

"I know a song about someone named Michael. Do you want me to sing it to you?" His face lit up.

"Dat your guitar?" he said, pointing to the black case in the corner.

"It sure is," I said. "Do you want me to play, Dotsie?"

"Yes, sing that song about Michael." I launched into "Michael (Row the Boat Ashore)" and Michael seemed to like it, tapping his foot after a while, and grinning. When a nurse walked in and saw the guitar, she said, "Don't leave that here. It's not safe." I didn't like to think that someone unprincipled could have access to my daughter's room, and feelings of helplessness washed over me, blending in with the pain until I felt so crushed I didn't think I could control myself. But I did, and stayed with Dotsie until after supper when she was ready to go to sleep. If the hospital had allowed it, I would have camped out by her bed for the night. As I walked down the hall, I passed Michael standing by the nurses' station and wondered why he was going to live and my child was not, and how there could possibly be a God in Heaven who could allow so much suffering.

After I got home and put Georgie to bed, I called my friend Lee on the telephone. Her husband, Arthur, answered, and before I said anything more than hello, he said, "Is it Dotsie?"

"Yes, she has leukemia." He had known through Dr. Weeks that it was a possibility. Dr. Weeks told me not to tell anyone the truth about Dotsie's illness, to keep it a secret as much as possible as she felt it would be destructive to Dotsie if everyone knew. My mother, however, had told all the members of our dramatic club and many of them trooped over from Manhattan to start our blood bank. Every time I turned around during the next few days, there was another old friend with her sleeve rolled up. But I tried to keep my Brooklyn Heights community, of which Dotsie was so much a part, in the dark. I didn't have the maturity or the wisdom to know that Dr. Weeks's advice was wrong. My tendency was always to obey the doctor, and so I went underground like a mole, pulling the terrible secret over me like so much dirt.

Bill and I tried to adjust, struggling with our grief while taking care of Georgie. We knew that it was only a matter of time before we would have to begin to face Georgie's problems along with her sister's. I spent the mornings working compulsively on my book, and submitted it before the month was out. Although I had taken to heart Dr. Weeks's suggestion of maintaining secrecy, I finally had to tell my closest friends. After two weeks Vicki and Lyn, the two people I had seen the most of in the last year, knew all the details. Their support meant everything to me, and the fact we still could get together with them and their husbands for dinner made all the difference.

In March, two months after the diagnosis, a friend of my mother's offered us her house in Sarasota for a month. Bill's parents treated us to the airfare, and Dotsie, Georgie, and I took off, with everybody saying it would be a great break to spend April outside, away from all the germs. Dotsie's immune system was affected by the disease and by the drugs, and her resistance to infection was low.

Just before I left, I bumped into my obstetrician on Montague Street in Brooklyn Heights. It was a gray March day, and I was delighted to see her comforting, stocky form bustling down the street against the wind like Mrs. Tiggywinkle.

"Hello there," she said, but without the usual twinkle in her eye. "How's Georgie?"

"Georgie's fine, physically, but she's still extremely withdrawn. There really hasn't been any change since I last talked to you." Remembering that self-incriminating conversation, which had taken place just after I'd read the reviews of *The Empty Fortress*, I took a deep breath. "Are you sure she wasn't affected somehow by the placenta previa? I can't shake the feeling that she suffered some kind of brain damage from anoxia."

"We talked about that before," she said, her tone harsh and abrupt. "You said her problems were environmental." The look on her face shifted to one of concern and compassion as she asked, "How's your other little girl? I understand she has leukemia. Dr. Weeks told me at the hospital." Evidently Dr. Weeks could tell the world if she felt like it.

"The chemotherapy's working," I said.

"How's it going? How are you doing with it?" I appreciated that she seemed to care about my emotional state.

"Oh, I'm crying a lot. I cry all the time."

"Oh, well, you can't do that. Here, let me give you something." She wrote out a prescription for five milligrams of Librium every four hours, said good-bye, and I was off to the drugstore.

In Florida we tried to have a good time. The house was beautiful and the beach lovely. Although Dotsie had blown up like a balloon on a drug called Prednisone, she was responding well to Mercaptopurine, her first anticancer drug. She had lost her hair, and the beautiful little girl of four months ago was now an overweight, bald, hurting five-year-old who was nevertheless game for anything and full of energy. After a week, she jumped in the pool without her bubble on, and as I prepared for the rescue, she came up swimming. It was a wonderful moment. Life was going on, she was learning and growing. Georgie was too, as she decided to give up her diapers without a struggle the same week. Georgie was not yet three, and I was proud of how quickly and easily she'd caught on, without any of the resistance her sister had shown.

One day I left the girls with a baby-sitter for a few hours while I went shopping, and when I got home, the sitter was in tears. "I can't find her," she said. She was sixteen years old and panic-stricken.

"Can't find who?"

"Georgie! Georgie's gone."

"How long ago did she disappear?" I kept my tone measured in an effort to quell her hysteria.

"An hour." She was trembling as she stood before me, probably expecting me to fly into a rage or fall apart. She looked so vulnerable all I could do was reassure her.

"I bet I know where she is," I said. Knowing Georgie, and her love of looking at water, I figured she'd followed the path by the lagoon. Because she was surefooted and didn't like to do more than wade, I didn't think she'd fallen in. "Come on, let's go find her. We'll all go." I set off with the sitter and Dotsie following. Sure enough, as we rounded a turn a few hundred yards from the house, there was Georgie, dressed only in her cotton bikini bottoms, down on her haunches with her back to us and playing with a wildflower. When I raced up to her and grabbed her, hugging her in relief, she leaned away from my arms, bending sideways and hanging her head as she trailed the flower from her hand. I explained to the sitter that Georgie was an extremely careful child and had never gotten herself into any kind of trouble, so it was only logical to assume that she had known what she was doing, young as she was.

After I'd been in Florida for two weeks, taking my Librium on schedule, I suddenly felt the need to invoke the tradition of cocktail hour. It was only civilized, I told myself, and highly appropriate under the circumstances. With my problems, who could blame me. Bill called me at this point and abruptly and mysteriously asked me to come home. I was bubbling over with the news of Georgie suddenly using the bathroom and Dotsie learning to swim and couldn't imagine why he kept telling me with such tension in his voice that I had to come home. What could possibly be prompting him to make such an uncharacteristic and outrageous request? I kept him on the phone for half an hour, trying to get him to tell me, but he wouldn't. For some reason I didn't even try to guess, and didn't play games with him because he sounded so serious. I couldn't believe he was being so dictatorial and secretive. "I have to stay," I told him, explaining that I couldn't renege on my housesitting obligation because there wasn't anybody else to take care of the house.

On May first I flew home with the children and Bill met me at the airport. Two things struck me as strange. One, he brought Vicki with him, and two, I somehow wound up sitting in the back seat with all four children, hers and mine. Vicki and her husband were close friends, and their baby was my godchild, but although I liked their children very much, I would have preferred to be in the front seat with my husband.

In Florida, I had put a blond streak in my hair to accentuate my tan, and although I thought I looked better than ever, Bill and Vicki ganged up on me in the car. They said the streak was awful and I'd have to get rid of it. Thinking they must be right, I let it pass and switched my thinking to getting home, to springtime in Brooklyn Heights (always my favorite season there) and to being in the Follies again. Although I could only manage being in the chorus this year, I wanted to be at the rehearsals with my friends.

Right after we got back, Georgie developed a fever and, I suspected, an ear infection. I took her in to Dr. Weeks's office. "She's had several ear infections, hasn't she," the doctor said as she looked at her chart. "Has she been coughing?" I said no. She looked at me carefully, watching me, and then said, "Are you concerned about Georgie not talking?" She spoke as if she were trying to handle me with kid gloves.

"No," I said. Denial is an amazing thing. No, of course not, Dr. Weeks. Who, me? "I think it's just because of all the strain of Dotsie. She'll be okay."

"She *is* almost three," said Dr. Weeks. "Please let me know if you have any concerns about it." I promised I would, got the prescription for Georgie's antibiotic, and left as quickly as I could.

Soon after that, I got a phone call from Lee asking if Georgie and Will, her little boy, could play together once a week. We set it up for the following Thursday.

Lee arrived and I was happy as always to see her. Not only was she a bright and witty writer, having proven herself by creating the Follies, but she was always cheerful and funny and ready with a pat on the back. Will looked just like her, tall, sturdy, and round, with pink cheeks and twinkly blue eyes.

She left Will off, and I took the two kids upstairs to Georgie's room to play. I sat there for a while to make sure Will had gotten used to everything, and then went down to do some laundry. As I left, he was going over to the shelf, where he picked up Dotsie's old jack-in-the-box and began to turn the handle. I could hear it as I went downstairs to the kitchen, making its annoying "bink, bink, bink" sound as he cranked out, "All around the mulberry bush the monkey chased the weasel." Georgie had never wanted to play with it but Will played it over and over again. Suddenly I heard a blood-curdling scream. I tore up the stairs to Georgie's room and there they were, sitting on the floor, Georgie with the jack-in-the-box on her lap, and Will holding his head with both hands. There was blood seeping through his fingers. I pried them loose and could see an ugly black-edged wound puckering up on his scalp. This was Georgie's first hostile act, and coincidentally the very first time she had actually interacted with another child.

Lee came over later that afternoon with Will bandaged up. He'd had to have four stitches and she got straight to the point. "I simply must talk to you about Georgie," she said.

"Come on in, we can sit on the sofa," I said, trying to be cordial and casual. Will stood by his mother's knee, unwilling to risk another encounter with Georgie, while Georgie and Dotsie sat on the floor doing puzzles. Dotsie was off Prednisone, her weight had returned to normal, and she was wearing a wig. She was in solid remission, and except for her pallor, she seemed almost normal. I leaned back against the cushions, trying to look relaxed, while Lee sat bolt upright.

"You have *got* to do something about Georgie. There is something wrong with her." She obviously had no doubts, and in spite of her frankness, her tone of voice was so gentle and concerned that it softened the blow. I knew she only wanted to help.

"You mean because she hit Will over the head with the jack-in-the-box? You mean she's abnormally hostile?" She sighed and looked at me with exasperation.

"No, anybody who's two could do that, I guess. Although I'm sorry it had to be Will who got hurt." She reached down and pulled him onto her lap, and I envied the way he nestled against her and twisted his head around to glance up at her for comfort. "No, it's more her lack of talking and the fact that she won't look at you that concerns me. And there was something about the house of cards she built at my house that gave me a clue." Georgie loved building extremely elaborate card houses, and was on grown-up level in her ability to construct them.

"Children like Georgie often have unusual capabilities along with their difficulties," she said. I didn't know what she was driving at, linking Georgie's problems with her unusual abilities. But the next sentence was all too clear. "I think she ought to be seen by a specialist." Even though I'd known it was coming, I felt exposed and desperate.

"You mean by a child psychiatrist."

"Yes." It was a relief, in a way, to have it out in the open, and to be prodded into action.

I sat up straight and said, "Okay, I'll make an appointment. Maybe Dr. Weeks can suggest somebody."

Lee set Will on the floor and stood up to go. She gave me a "I know you can handle it even though it's rough" look.

"Let me know what happens," she said, giving me a quick hug. I envied her again as Will reached up his hand and willingly invited her to hold it as they went out the door.

Chapter 3

Dr. Small

I made an appointment with a child psychiatrist recommended by Dr. Weeks. At least now we were going to know what we were dealing with, and we could come up with a plan of action.

Bill and I took both girls with us as we thought the doctor might want to see the whole family. It was June, so Brooklyn Heights must have been blooming as we walked down to his office, but life had become flat, and the geraniums and the sycamores had lost their charm. Dr. Singer was friendly and professional as he sat behind his big desk with a studied casualness. He watched Georgie as she roamed around riffling magazine pages, brushing her fingers against the base of a lamp, and handling plastic blocks in a basket in the corner. She cruised, absorbing the room with her senses, but wouldn't come to the doctor or look at him, and only reluctantly allowed her hand to be held at arm's length. She came to rest after a while near the window. She sat with her legs out in a V, hunched over a metal top which she spun repeatedly. She looked as if she were mesmerized by its colors as it whirred into solid red and slowed into stripes again.

Acting as if it didn't matter what he said in front of her, as if she weren't capable of understanding, Dr. Singer gave us his diagnosis: "Your daughter is autistic. It is, as you know, a very severe disturbance. An emotional disturbance."

"Emotional? She's emotionally disturbed?" I hated the sound of it, and it bore out everything I'd read about Bettelheim and his theories. At that moment, as frozen in time as I was during Dotsie's diagnosis, only the pain of my empathy for Georgie outweighed my embarrassment and shame. "Yes," he said. "Severely disturbed with some autistic features." I felt weighed down as I sat there remembering what I had read in *The Empty Fortress* and its reviews. How could I live with myself if I believed that autism was "a defense against unbearable anxiety" and "the source of this anxiety is not an organic impairment [as I stubbornly persisted in believing], but the child's evaluation of the conditions of his life as being utterly destructive." After Dotsie's illness was diagnosed, I could believe Bettelheim even more easily. Georgie was just responding to a destructive atmosphere—first, unhappily married parents, and then her only sibling who was dying. An article I'd seen recently on the psychosomatic factors in cancer was the clincher. Both my children were *electing* to disappear. And now Dr. Singer, kind though he was, was making me feel that perhaps I *was* somehow at fault. I wondered just what kind of emotional ray gun I possessed, and exactly how I used it.

"What can we do?" I asked. Bill sat there, his chin in his hand, looking as if he accepted and respected the doctor's opinion.

"There's a special school I can refer you to, in the East New York section of Brooklyn. About an hour from here."

"A special school. An hour away," I said. "Well, we have a lot to think about. Do you want to see Dotsie, too?" She was in the waiting room looking at books and playing with toys, probably glad that Georgie was in with the doctor and not her.

"No, I understand that except for her illness she's fine." That was nice to hear, and I wasn't about to bring up the relationship of cancer to repressed rage. I preferred to believe that my daughter was dying because a cure for leukemia hadn't yet been discovered, and wondered if measles, diphtheria, whooping cough, tetanus, po-

lio, and smallpox had been blamed on repressed rage before the age
of vaccinations. "But I would like to see both you and your husband
separately," the doctor said.

Several days later, Dotsie and Georgie were upstairs taking a
bath while Bill and I talked in the living room. He had come home
and had changed into comfortable clothes and was just getting started
on his sherry. My own need for a drink every night had passed
when I got home from Florida. I had always been afraid of daily
drinking and particularly scared of drowning my sorrows. Besides,
I was taking Librium, and wasn't supposed to combine alcohol with
the tranquilizer.

Usually we confined our conversation to the mundane events
of the day, but so much tension had accumulated between us since
I'd returned from Florida that I wanted to clear the air. I found
myself confessing that I'd developed a romantic interest in a cast
member of the Follies and had even met him a few times for a walk
on the Promenade. I told Bill I was sorry, that I knew it was wrong
and bad for the marriage, and that I wasn't going to see him anymore.
He said, "Well, I wouldn't feel too guilty about it because Vicki
and I have been seeing each other. It started when you were in
Florida. I tried to tell you."

Suddenly several things became clear: why she was in the front
seat of the car on the way home from the airport, and why she
hadn't been able to tell me what was bothering her when I'd gone
over to her apartment several times lately to "cheer her up."

"Is this why you wanted me to come home early from Florida?"
I asked. "Did you feel it was getting out of control?"

"Yes," he said.

"And did it?" I asked.

"Yes."

"Why didn't you just come straight out and tell me?"

"We didn't think you could handle it," he said. This killed me.
It smacked of conspiracy and superiority. And what did they think
they were doing by fooling around in the first place? Was that
protecting me? My whole world collapsed like one of Georgie's card

houses as he said gravely, as if to give it dignity, "I've fallen in love with her. I couldn't help myself."

It turned out they were right—I couldn't handle it. I thought about it for a couple of weeks, and tried to talk to Vicki about it. I told her it had never occurred to me that she was carrying on with my husband because I thought she would have told me straight out. After all, this was the sophisticated sixties, when open marriage sounded just great, as long as there was *trust* and *no subterfuge*. All our friends had been talking about it and arguing pro and con. Talk is cheap, I was finding, and open marriage was an oxymoron. I wanted no part of it.

When I told Bill that he would either have to give her up or get out, I fully expected him to say he would end the relationship. Not for one second did I think he would actually leave. But leave he did, and his parting words were, "I can't live a lie anymore," as he opened the door and strode away with his head held high. Live a lie? Didn't he care about us at all? And didn't he realize he was like a fireman leaving his own burning house? Evidently not, because by the time I had collected myself, he was already halfway to the corner, walking fast in the dark red pants I'd bought and hemmed for him, and which I had ironed that morning. I let him go, thinking I could never, ever forgive either one of them for their betrayal and their failure to support me when I needed them most. I felt I was being left for dead.

We saw Dr. Singer separately a week later. He told me I was a strong person, and was going to be able to cope with my problems. But he said that Bill was untreatable. He said he was pathologically withdrawn and unreachable, had no interest in changing his attitudes or behavior, and had been damaged emotionally in his childhood. He said I shouldn't expect much from him, that Bill was incapable of a healthy relationship.

*   *   *

They say when you go through hell you find out who your friends are. In my case, many of my friends deserted me because I was suddenly a single mother and because we all bought into Bettelheim and thought I must have been unloving in some subtle but fundamental way. Vicki, who had left her husband and was living with Bill, said as much one night when I called her in tears, begging her to let Bill come home. "You didn't know how to love him," she said. All I could think of was all those cheese soufflés I'd baked! Not to mention his favorite Japanese and Chinese food I'd learned to cook, the pants I'd pressed every weekday morning, the books about marriage I'd bought and tried to learn from, and the huge emotional investment I'd made in our life together. Did I have it all wrong? I guessed I did because everything was such a mess. Some of it had to be my fault.

With Bill gone, my precarious self-esteem took a nose-dive, and my self-pity knew no bounds. My list of personal negatives got longer every day: I was too self-centered, too critical, too controlling, too depressed, too serious, too immature, too burned out, too angry, too tired. I yearned, positively clamored, for affection and reassurance, for someone to tell me, even if it wasn't true, that everything was going to be all right. I found myself skating across my days, taking more tranquilizers, and finally, getting into the scotch again at night. I kept thinking about how my brother Johnny used to kid me when he thought I was being a pest. He could always get my attention by saying, "I pity the poor man who marries *you*." Maybe he hadn't been kidding after all, and I was getting exactly what I deserved.

Georgie deteriorated that summer, her symptoms becoming exaggerated and more bizarre. On a hot day in August, when we went to the zoo in Central Park, she couldn't take her eyes off the seals and suddenly began to imitate them. She looked as if she wanted to merge with them as she gripped the iron railing. The wonder of it was that she imitated them so perfectly. I couldn't understand why she wouldn't imitate human noises and begin to talk. She was so fascinated, we had to pry her loose from the railing when we left to go to the merry-go-round. And when the merry-go-round music became audible a few minutes later, she pulled back, and we practically had to drag her to the ticket window. Dotsie scrambled for the largest outside horse she could find, while I lifted Georgie up on a small brown one and buckled the strap. I stood on the sidelines, inexplicably moved to tears as I'd always been by the grinding, tinny music and the children riding by. Dotsie waved as she passed me, poised and self-possessed, but Georgie stared straight ahead, grimacing as she clutched the pole, her eyes squinting in little crescents.

In the fall, Georgie went to nursery school at our church and Dotsie, when she was able to go, went to kindergarten in the local public school. The special school suggested by Dr. Singer was an hour away and in the opposite direction from Memorial Sloan-Kettering, where Dotsie was being treated. Since Georgie was too young to go on a school bus, I didn't see how I could get her there. I just hoped, through the haze of my denial, that somehow regular nursery school would be enough. I had all I could do to cope with Dotsie who, at this stage, was often out of remission.

And Georgie's teacher inundated her with affection, sure she could elicit a response as she was such a warm, caring person. But Georgie just sat there as oblivious as ever, not caring where she was, on a lap or a floor. It was all the same to her. The teachers let her stay only out of kindness and told me she was getting nothing out of it.

In January our landlord came downstairs and announced that we would have to move because his sister needed our apartment for herself. I was so glad to get out of our rundown duplex into something sunny and practical, I could hardly wait to move. With the help of our next-door neighbors, we were in our new place by February. Right after that, a little magazine called *Guideposts*, put out by Norman Vincent Peale, began to arrive in the mail. Some kind person had subscribed to it for me although I never found out who. Sometimes the stories in it were sappy, and written in an emotional style I'd been trained to disdain, but I found them inspiring in spite of the schmaltz. One column, called "His Mysterious Ways," had stories of amazing coincidences and happenings that convinced people that God was present in their lives. It still never occurred to me to actively pray unless I was in church or putting the children to bed, but I was definitely getting interested in exploring spirituality after reading all these stories of altered lives.

The new apartment seemed to throw Georgie completely. She would endlessly line up her little colored pegboard pegs in long, undulating rows across the room. She began to spin in one specific corner, standing there with her eyes rolling up into her head and her hands clamped to her sides. She would spin for half an hour at a time if I didn't stop her, making a soft eerie warbling sound.

Soon after we moved, I was introduced to the headmaster of a local private school who agreed to take Georgie but wanted her evaluated first by a friend of his, a psychiatrist in Manhattan. I made an appointment, thinking that with some counseling and special attention, Georgie would surely be able to go to a regular school. I was in for a rude and final awakening.

Derek Small, M.D., practiced psychiatry from an office on the Upper East Side near Fifth Avenue. Bill, of whom I had seen little in the last nine months, met us at the doctor's office. He looked as elegant as always in his pin-striped suit, French cuffs, and shiny black shoes, especially in contrast to our bedraggled little group. Dotsie was by now obviously ill, with another hair loss and a faintly brownish tinge to her skin. Georgie was spacey and more jittery than ever, and I was drained and tense. I had on one of my Brooklyn Heights housewife outfits: parka, denim skirt, and flats. I couldn't help thinking he was doing better from this than I was. I had brought Dotsie along because she had an appointment at Memorial Sloan-Kettering for a transfusion.

In the doctor's office Georgie displayed all her symptoms. She had deteriorated in the ten months since Dr. Singer had seen her although she had become even lovelier-looking. As is typical of autistic children, she was exceptionally beautiful, with her blue eyes offset by dark lashes, and her hair a mass of silky curls. While Georgie roamed around the periphery of the room in constant motion, Dotsie sat immobile on her father's lap, as if her very stillness would keep him with her. Bill and I faced the doctor across three feet of open space as Dr. Small probably felt it was therapeutically advantageous to forgo the barrier of his desk.

"There is no question in my mind that your daughter is disturbed," he said. "She is an autistic child, and she is also retarded." No one had said the word *retarded* in my presence before, and I couldn't stand hearing it. Somehow I had clung to the notion that Georgie's intelligence was in the normal range. *Retarded* sounded final and absolute and I reacted with desperate disbelief.

"But if she's retarded, why was she able to learn to tie her shoes when she was barely two?"

Dr. Small looked exasperated and ignored my question. "She is obviously retarded and low functioning, and a great deal of it is due to the fact that *you*"—he looked straight at me—"have avoided contact with her." The words *avoided contact* hit me like bullets but I tried to fight on. Actually I would have preferred bullets.

"Isn't there some organic or neurological impairment involved in her retardation?" He looked at me as if I were trying to cop out.

"No," he replied. "And if you have any doubts, I'll prove it to you by admitting her to Rusk Institute for a complete evaluation. It will involve every test there is for brain damage and neurological impairment but I can guarantee you that they will find no organic impairment in your child."

"Okay, let's have her admitted to Rusk Institute." I didn't believe him. I *knew* there was brain damage, and surely they would find it. I heard Bill sigh with resignation. He felt this was just one more exercise of my futile, crazy attitudes, just as having Dotsie treated at Sloan-Kettering was. He had felt strongly that Brooklyn Hospital was good enough, and that Sloan-Kettering amounted to heroic measures.

It was a relief to be outside even though the March wind,

potentiated by downdrafts and tall buildings, blasted us on our way to the bus. We stood at the bus stop with our coats flapping and Dotsie put her hand on her head to make sure her wig didn't blow off. Georgie strained at my hand as she looked up at the branches of the tree next to us. The bus rolled to the curb and I nudged the girls up the steps, turning to say good-bye to Bill. He grabbed my arm, looked at me pointedly, and said, "Let Dotsie die, institutionalize Georgie, and get on with your life."

I watched him stonily as he disappeared around the corner onto Madison Avenue. I would never agree with him or give up, I thought. There were the girls, sitting demurely in the back, Dotsie wedging Georgie in next to the window, knowing her responsibility for containing Georgie's urges to wander. How I loved them both. And nobody was going to convince me that Bill was right. I *was* getting on with my life—my children were my life—and I knew I would fight to the finish for both of them. There were several battles going on here, and who knows, maybe I'd win one.

Sloan-Kettering took up a whole city block, its pale red brick and single-paned windows looking solid, modern, and innocuous, a kind of poor relation to the soaring gothic whiteness of New York Hospital looming up to the northeast. Dotsie had made a place for herself at Memorial, as she called it, and enjoyed it as an adjunct community in spite of its associations with pain and disease. We went up in the elevator, checked in at the pediatric section, and settled down in the small, windowless outpatient waiting room. A tall, poorly dressed boy, emaciated and bald, with track marks from IVs on his arms, sat with his mother opposite us.

When our doctor, Bettina Merrill, appeared, peeking around the door with a welcoming smile, we were glad as always to see her. She was petite and vibrant, with short auburn hair swept away from a heart-shaped face, her brown eyes warm and concerned, and her small diamond earrings twinkling. She added a certain upbeat glamour, a dose of Texas charm, to the oppressively sad surroundings of the pediatric service. Her understanding and sensitivity had saved me from putting myself on a complete guilt trip over leukemia. She had shaken her head at my suggestion of possible contributing factors, smiling at my silliness in a comforting way. She explained that leukemia was a riddle and that sometimes, as in Dotsie's case, there was no clue as to its cause. There were often genetic factors, and factors to do with poisons in the environment. She explained that until someone came up with a vaccine or a cure, people were going to speculate about the etiology and blame themselves if they could. She reassured me every time I saw her. She had seen us through all the difficult phases of treatment like the bone marrow tests, the endless blood work, and the side effects of the drugs Dotsie took. Dr. Merrill said it was hard to hang on to your humanity on the pediatric floor. She was going to leave the service and study psychiatry because she felt that Georgie's problems needed addressing even more than Dotsie's because they would last for a full lifetime of tragedy.

While Dotsie was hooked up to an IV for the medicine she was receiving that day, the social worker for the pediatric service asked me if I'd like to talk. I said yes, then found myself crying inconsolably in her little white office. She told me that an agency called Cancer Care would be willing to provide me with a housekeeper if I thought it would help. I perked up instantly, thinking it would be very helpful indeed, and hired someone the next day. She was just the right person—a calm, stolid, capable Jamaican woman who looked as if she could take a Martian invasion in stride. One of my friends commented acidly after she arrived, "Well, you finally have what you always wanted—full-time help." Another "friend," whom I had known well in college, also had a strange reaction to my trials. She said she was furious with me for messing up my life to such an extent, as if I'd concocted it all on my own. These people, whose misplaced anger had blocked their empathy and also, conveniently, relieved them of the responsibility of helping me, faded from my life, while the relationships with the many old friends who stuck by me were deepened and strengthened.

* * *

Dr. Small arranged to have Georgie admitted to Rusk Institute a
week later. I caught my breath when we entered the lobby, I was
so impressed by its soaring elegance and the enormous greenhouse
at the back filled with exotic plants and foliage. It was quite a change
from the squatness of Sloan-Kettering with its plastic chairs and
relentless philodendrons. I wished I could find a spot among the
orchids and the frangipani and stay there, forever avoiding the task
ahead.

Georgie cast her eyes up to the ceiling and warbled faintly as
we rode up in the elevator to the floor where she would be admitted.
When a nurse met us and showed us her room, I was relieved to
see that it had several beds in it, and colorful curtains and bed-
spreads. The common room, where the occupational therapy took
place, was bright and full of toys and materials for artwork and
crafts. There were no other patients in evidence. Although she didn't
seem to mind being left, and the nurses were so nice that I was sure
she would be well taken care of, I could hardly bear to hand over
her little overnight bag. It had a nightmare quality but there would
be no waking up with relief.

When I visited the next day, I found Georgie sitting on the
floor in the common room, spinning a top. When I went to her and
hugged her, she responded by looking obliquely toward the window.
As a child who was physically intact, she was completely out of
place among the other children in the room. A girl of about fifteen
wandered aimlessly, chewing gum and chatting with the nurses,
trying to look nonchalant about the two steel hooks which now
served as her hands. In an attempt to commit suicide, she had lost
both arms at the elbow when she jumped in front of a subway train.
A younger child, this one with no arms at all, just a torso ending
in flippers, was holding a paintbrush in one of her toelike appen-
dages. She was a thalidomide baby who smiled perpetually, not
understanding what your problem was if you felt sorry for her—
she had always been like that. There were other children deformed
to various degrees, some with cerebral palsy, some who were neu-

rologically impaired. What was my little imp of a Georgie doing here? How could it possibly be appropriate? And surely it must be damaging to expose her to all these children with their frightening disabilities. It was all I could do not to scoop her up and run. But what I hoped was wisdom prevailed, and instead, I sat with her awhile on the floor, borrowing her top and spinning it, trying to give her something just by being there. She didn't seem to notice the other children, and was as self-absorbed as ever. I didn't stay long.

Although Dr. Small had said that Georgie would be at Rusk for two to six weeks, the doctor in charge was ready to discharge her in ten days. He was a warm, cozy, big-hearted man, but was nevertheless mercilessly emphatic in his diagnosis. "She has absolutely no physical or neurological impairment whatsoever," he said. "There is no brain damage." He couldn't understand why I harped so much on brain damage, and I couldn't convince him that Georgie had been autistic from birth. I felt he was pointing the finger at me, accusing me of driving my child crazy, and criticizing me for not appreciating the fact that she was free of brain damage. I got the feeling he thought I had a ghoulish streak, as if, along with all my other reprehensible qualities, I would wish something as horrendous as brain damage on my child.

Before he discharged Georgie, he took me down the hall and introduced me to a doctor who would be able to suggest a workable treatment plan, someone who knew something about autism. We met in a small, cold, gray box of a space with nothing in it but a white table and two chairs. The doctor, in her mid-forties, had black hair, dark eyes, and a serious, intelligent face. Although she was sensitive to the gravity of the situation, her manner was colloquial and casual. She was studying Georgie's chart with a pencil in her hand when I walked in, and she looked up, motioning me to the remaining chair. As soon as I sat down, she told me without mincing words that the best place for Georgie's treatment was Bellevue, in the experimental unit for autistic children. "If you can stand Bellevue," she added, looking resigned and raising her eyebrows.

"Of course I can stand Bellevue if it's the best place," I said bravely. It didn't *feel* like the best place. It felt like the end of the world. Bellevue meant the madhouse, bedlam, bars on the windows, cockroaches, crime, terrified, terrifying people, antipsychotic drugs like Thorazine, dark, grim architecture, locked wards, paper slippers, rattling keys, and sadistic nurses. People said you only went there DOA. But I would trust this doctor. She said that in the autistic unit there were only nine children to twenty-two staff, that the area was large, bright, and clean, that Georgie would be worked with constantly, and that she would come home on the weekends.

"Come home on the weekends?" I couldn't believe she was saying this. "*Only* on the weekends?" She stressed the desperate need for early intervention in the treatment of autism, twenty-four hours a day in a neutral setting. Without it, Georgie would have virtually no chance.

After receiving this "referral," I was on the point of collapse. But I managed to pick Georgie up with her suitcase and get us home. In a daze I tried to absorb the fact that my child, soon to be four, was to go to Bellevue to live among a group of psychotic children in the possibly vain hope that she might improve and progress to the point where she could lead a meaningful existence. I tried to console myself and to marshal some gratitude. She was not being consigned to oblivion and deterioration. There was every chance that she would grow in the Bellevue program, and that was the point. I would hang on to that, but it was going to be hard. I felt like someone huddling in a dark tent with a hurricane brewing outside.

Chapter 4

Freedom

Although I kept looking for silver linings, my life became a joyless push, an honoring of responsibilities, a grim slog through each day in order to do my duty and see it all through. I'd started seeing a psychiatrist for half a session a week, and he didn't have many answers for me. In fact, I had the feeling he didn't think I was going to survive. He kept offering to increase the dosage of my Librium, and I kept taking him up on it, until I was taking the maximum allowed by law. My druggist always gave me twice the number of pills free of charge but I didn't tell the doctor for fear he'd cut me back. In addition, I was downing several stiff drinks every night after I put the children to bed. My mother, who said I'd begun to sound fuzzy when she talked to me on the telephone, tried to help, but she worked full-time and had developed Parkinson's disease the year before Georgie was born. My brother Johnny and his wife had three small children and lived hundreds of miles away. My brother David and his wife, Carol, lived nearby, and were concerned about my tranquilizer consumption too, but they felt almost as helpless in the face of all the tragedy as I did. My self-confidence was so shaken, and my grief was so intense, that I'd walled myself in with defenses. "God help you," someone said to me on the street one day when I presented her with my list of difficulties. Even going to church had lost its meaning. I felt that if I stood up in the middle of a service and screamed, nobody would pay any attention, it was such a somber, formal place. I was enduring my own version of Vietnam, in a personal war so unpopular that it seemed almost indecent to survive it. I would gladly have traded places with Dotsie.

One night in June, a few weeks after my thirtieth birthday, I settled down for an evening of television when I realized there was nothing in the house to drink. I couldn't seem to relax, and within two hours had taken five tranquilizers, all that was left in the bottle. In an unconscious bid for attention, I called my psychiatrist. He panicked, thinking suicide. He didn't know the druggist had been doubling my prescription, so he didn't think I could handle such a large quantity. He told me I must arrange to have two friends spend the night with me to make sure I'd be all right, which I did although I thought it was ridiculous.

The next morning I woke up feeling as if I'd deliberately wound all the strings of my guitar to the point where they snapped. My friends went home to sleep and gave my family a chance to come to my rescue. My mother and my brother David arrived to sit on the sofa with me while I cried on their shoulders. I hadn't seen Bill for months, and he came over, too, but all I could do was lambaste him for deserting us. After he left, the emotional pain built to the point where I was willing to do anything to take it away. I ran into the bathroom, locked the door, and downed a handful of over-the-counter sleeping pills which I'd heard couldn't kill you no matter how many you took. I only hoped they'd dull the pain to the point where I could stop crying and start functioning. They worked only too well, rendering me dangerously close to passing out. After that, I didn't care what happened to me: when my mother consulted with my psychiatrist and decided I should be hospitalized, I raised no objection. I was at the bottom of a slide innocently begun fifteen months ago on the day I'd accepted my obstetrician's offer of a prescription for tranquilizers. The palliatives hadn't worked in the long run. I guess they never do.

* * *

At the hospital, I was given a physical by a young intern who looked at me quizzically over horn-rimmed glasses as if to say, "Are you sure you absolutely have to be here?" I was admitted to the evaluation ward, and issued a seersucker bathrobe, a nightgown, and paper slippers. That night I was given some liquid medicine in a paper cup. "It's paraldehyde, honey, you gonna love it," the nurse said. I retired to my room, grateful that my roommate appeared to be catatonic, and I was asleep in five minutes.

The next morning I woke up refreshed and clear-headed and eager to go home, realizing that this dreary, frightening place was not what I'd had in mind at all. When I'd visited a college friend who'd had a nervous breakdown, her room had been colorful and cheerful, not a drab cell like this one with an unopenable window. My roommate wasn't very helpful either, as she lay in bed like a corpse. In fact, I checked to make sure she was breathing before I put on my bathrobe and slippers and ventured out into the hallway looking for food. I found my way to the day room, where a large number of sedated women in nightclothes were quietly having breakfast. The room was vast, with windows on either side covered with impenetrable mesh, and a long cafeteria counter at the far end. I picked up a speckled plastic tray still hot and wet from the washer, was served a dollop of oatmeal, and cast around for a safe place to sit. There was an empty seat next to a teenager who was attractive and well groomed, and who looked intelligent and alert enough to carry on a conversation in spite of the gauze bandages on her wrists. I introduced myself and asked her what she thought of the hospital.

"Oh, it's all right. As long as you don't make any trouble."

"Make any trouble?"

"Yeah, then you go up to the flight deck."

"The flight deck?"

"Yeah, where they put you in a straitjacket and strap you in a wheelchair." She smiled.

"How do I get out of here?" I asked.

"Ask the social worker. You'll see her, she'll be around a little later." When I had finished my breakfast, I deposited my tray in the pass-through, and approached the nurses' station. A nurse with a brutish face like a scone was leafing through some records, and after a while she looked up.

"May I please go back to my room?" I asked politely, hoping good manners would forestall a trip to the flight deck.

"No," she said. "No lying down in the daytime." I couldn't believe it. Not only was I penned in here like an animal, but I was to be allowed neither rest nor privacy. The disappointment in my face failed to move the nurse.

"Take these," she said, handing me some pills and a cup of water. I took them obediently and she resumed her work. I wandered back into the day room. The tables had been moved to the side, and a group of women were moving in a circle in the freed space in the center. They shuffled together with their heads down, their paper slippers swishing on the linoleum, until one of the women suddenly raised her fist and shouted an obscenity at the ceiling. Every few seconds she repeated the action, while the rest of the women silently circled around with their heads down, playing slow-motion ring-around-the-rosy. I was dumbfounded. I'd never seen anything like it, not even in the movies. There was a small table against the wall with two chairs near it, and I sat in one of them. Should I try to make the best of it now that I was here? A nurse's aide rustled over and sat down opposite me.

"How are you feeling today?" she asked kindly. She was pretty and petite, with a faint Spanish accent.

"Fine, thanks. How are you?" I said, trying to smile.

"Fine, thank you." She looked away absently. I had an idea.

"Uh, do you play bridge?" I always thought people played bridge when they were in a psychiatric hospital. She jumped up.

"I go get the cards and you teach me, okay?" In a few minutes she brought back a beat-up, skimpy deck of cards. I counted them.

"This deck only has thirty-seven cards in it, I told her, trying to be kind in the face of her eagerness. She looked disappointed. I turned the cards over and noticed there were nothing but face cards.

"And it's a pinochle deck," I said. She looked embarrassed and upset. "Look," I tried to reassure her. "Don't worry about it. We'll learn bridge some other time. Thanks."

"You welcome," she said, getting up to leave. I sat there for a few more minutes, trying to decide what to do. I knew if I could just talk to my mother and tell her what this place was like, she'd come and get me out of here. I saw a nurse standing near the doorway, and thought she might be able to tell me where I could make a phone call. She was a large, authoritative woman with a puffy, angry face.

"Excuse me," I said. "Would you please tell me how I can make a phone call?" The question seemed to amuse as well as irritate her.

"What did you say?" she asked carefully, although I knew she'd heard me.

"I said I'd like to make a phone call."

She turned away from me, and raising her arms like a ballerina, she bellowed, "Now ladies! I want you all to stop moving for a moment. I want you all to listen to this." The shuffling ladies stopped and turned toward her. "This here lady wants to make a phone call. Did you hear me? This lady wants to make a phone call!" She shook her head, a tight smile of absolute power on her face, and I realized with a sense of violation and outrage that she had complete control over me. "Where you think you are, honey, jail?" She arched her back, turned, and walked away, glancing over her shoulder at me contemptuously while the ladies resumed their dance of death.

I stood there bewildered and degraded as I realized I'd been disenfranchised and was helpless in the hands of unprincipled people in a locked ward. I decided my best course of action would be to sit quietly and wait for the social worker, hoping she would be more reasonable than the guardian of the gulag.

Fifteen minutes later I saw the social worker. She was unmistakable—neutral and respectable in her neat gray suit and white blouse. When I told her I didn't think I needed to be in the hospital, she was polite and understanding and seemed to agree with me. "You can see the doctor this afternoon and discuss the possibility of being discharged." I felt a relief so great it was hard to contain myself. She said the doctor would see me at two o'clock.

I suffered through a lunch of macaroni and cheese and spongy carrots, all consumed with a spoon as other utensils were considered dangerous, and at two o'clock a nurse came and escorted me to the office of the psychiatrist who was the head of the unit. It was as bleak as a boxcar, with a filthy window in an awkward alcove, but the doctor himself was cheerful, appealing, and extremely good-looking. He looked casual and relaxed, his shirtsleeves rolled up to his elbows, and he tilted back in his chair and smiled as I came in. As soon as I sat down he said, "I understand you would like to be discharged." I nodded. "I'd like to ask you a few questions first." When he queried me about the quantities of tranquilizers and alcohol I'd grown accustomed to, he shook his head.

"Fifty milligrams of Librium every four hours, combined with alcohol. You were taking risks."

"I didn't know that, and I really thought I needed it. But I'll never take pills again. All I want to do is get out of here and take care of my children."

"Yes, well, I've spoken to your doctor, and I understand you have your hands full. I will discharge you if you can get someone to assume responsibility for you."

"You will? Just like that?" I could hardly believe my good fortune. "Can I make a phone call?" He said yes! By three o'clock that same afternoon, the key was turning in the lock behind me, and within minutes I was hailing a cab with my mother and we were headed for her apartment in Manhattan. She was taking me home for a rest. As soon as I was settled in her big four-poster bed with a glass of her most special carrot juice, she told me that Georgie was being admitted to Bellevue earlier than expected, and that Bill was handling it. "She'll be there tomorrow, and they don't want you to see her for three weeks because she needs to get used to it. Bill's taking care of Dotsie, and you're just supposed to rest and take vitamins."

I found I was able to give up tranquilizers with no problem, and cigarettes as well, but I began to drink more. When I went away to Connecticut for the Fourth of July weekend to visit an aunt and uncle, they noticed it and gave me a book to read called *The Search for Serenity*. The author seemed to understand what it felt like to live in a perpetual state of fear and despair. As I read the book, I began to feel less isolated. My uncle and I talked about it, and he lectured me about my drinking.

"I know a woman who lives near here," he said, "and even if she had a daughter with leukemia and another who was autistic, and her husband had left her for another woman, she would still smile when she said good morning."

"Baloney!" I said. But he persisted, advising me to stop drinking and go to a recovery group where I would learn how to change my attitudes. "It's not your problems that are killing you," he said. "It's your *response* to your problems." The word *response* resonated, offering me the option of survival. I decided to take his advice.

I took a train back to the city and found my car sitting on its tire rims, stripped. I left it there to be towed away, and wondered how I was going to manage my trips to my children's hospitals without a car.

When I got home, it seemed I'd been away for months instead of days, and my life felt as if it had turned around. Instead of living my life accommodating everyone else, I had a personal goal for the first time in years, and that was to stay out of the psychiatric hospital. Although I didn't think I could ever live it down, and would be forever shocked for having been in such a place, at least I could try never to go back. And that meant I would have to take better care of myself.

One morning, when Dotsie and I went to the playground, I saw a friend who had just gotten her Ph.D. in psychology. Dotsie ran off to the slide, and my friend and I had an intense conversation. I told her about my day in the hospital, and about my feelings of guilt over my children's illnesses. She told me that the degree of guilt was totally inappropriate and must stem from my childhood.

Shortly after that encounter, I became friends with a psychiatric nurse I met at one of the recovery group meetings my uncle had suggested I attend. She said I could think of my experience in the psychiatric ward as tantamount to an aversion treatment for insanity, that I'd hit bottom there, and could even be grateful for it because it had scared me into becoming teachable. We spent many long hours going over my entire childhood. I was virtually in therapy with her, and she, and others at the meetings I went to, helped me learn to live with myself more comfortably. I learned the value of staying in the moment, living "in the now because now is all you have," and it was like crawling into the eye of the hurricane. My self-esteem began to grow, and I began to find a commonality with people. Everywhere I went I had friendly encounters, and almost always, people were pleasant when I was. Prejudices, differences, snobbery, and elitism faded away, and I found I could link up with almost anyone. Clear-headed, and with my nervous system healing, I began to think I might be able to manage after all.

Chapter 5

Responses

When Georgie was admitted to Bellevue, she settled in without a hint of protest, and when her three weeks of adjustment were up, I went to the hospital to take her home for the weekend. I left Dotsie with my next-door neighbor, and took the subway into Manhattan, wishing I still had a car.

I walked down Thirtieth Street toward the hospital and could see the East River flowing sluggishly beyond the FDR Drive. I cringed, and shrank into my raincoat, hunching my shoulders and trying not to look up at the heavily barred windows of the prison ward on the second floor. My newly acquired knowledge of city hospitals wasn't helping, and I had to force myself to focus on the clean, organized, productive autistic unit on the sixth floor with its view of the river. I reminded myself that the unit wasn't really Bellevue, with its connotations of violence and indigence; it was the New York University–Bellevue Autistic Unit. It was not a corral where the disturbed vegetated, but a cheerful, organized place for therapy and healing, fully staffed and funded, with a high success rate.

Feeling oppressed and fragile, and awash in bad memories of my day in the "psycho ward," I swung open the heavy doors and crossed the dimly lit lobby as quickly as I could. The thick wire mesh covering the windows diffused the light coming through, and people were everywhere, a cross-section of humanity, people in white coats, people with badges, uniformed guards, patients. A squat woman in a kerchief was waiting for the elevator with several children in tow. Huddling among the folds of their mother's black skirt with their thumbs in their mouths, they looked up at me with round eyes.

The antiquated elevator took several minutes to come, the hand crawling maddeningly slowly counterclockwise on the circular brass indicator. As I rode up, two doctors stood next to me, one tall and pale, the other, small, fine-boned, and South American. They were chatting in low voices but I could hear every word. "Maria." The small one was speaking and smiling, looking up at the other, who was clutching a chart to his chest with both hands. "What are you going to do with Maria?" He was talking about a little girl in the autistic section, I was sure. I had met her when I visited the unit before Georgie was admitted. She was just Georgie's age. Beautiful, with shining wavy black hair, olive skin, and huge liquid black eyes, she pranced and skipped when she moved, drooling constantly and staring through everyone, unable to keep still. She had never spoken. The doctor raised his arm in a gesture of dismissal, flashing a large gold pinky ring with a diamond in it, and a jeweled cufflink as well. "I think we going to send her to Lourdes!" he said, making a joke. He laughed, his gold fillings glinting, the other doctor chuckled, and I wanted to bash their heads in.

I got off on six. I would have to run the gauntlet of the disturbed children's ward in order to get to the autistic unit, and the locked door to my right was the only access point. Its bright, primary color blue enamel was badly chipped by thousands of frantic attempts to summon someone from the other side with the big brass key that would fit the huge lock. I knocked and listened for the sound of approaching footsteps but heard only the cacophonous shouts of the children on the other side. Finally, I pounded with the heel of my hand, and then with my keys, contributing a few chips of my own.

After several minutes a tall, striking woman in street clothes opened the door and said, "Come this way," her long red fingernails glinting like rubies as she graciously ushered me in. "I'm Miss Dials," she said. Her perfect outfit and sparkling grooming proclaimed that she was part of the solution while I was part of the problem.

We walked along the perimeter of the day room of the ward, staying close to the wall. It teemed with older children, almost all boys. A group crowded around me, grabbing at my raincoat and the strap of my purse, asking me questions like "Where you goin'?" and "What you doin' here?" A slim, nervous boy of about ten brushed against me, his face tilting up at me six inches from my nose. He bobbed and wove, bursting with energy, unconsciously invading my space. I felt uncomfortable and scared, and guilty, because my heart should have been going out to him when, instead, all I wanted to do was get past him as fast as I could.

"Who you comin' for?" asked a taller boy, equally close and homing in from the other side. "You got somethin' for me?" I followed along behind Miss Dials, grateful for her presence as she shooed them away, calling some of them by name and glancing over her shoulder to make sure I was successfully fending them off.

"Oh these kids," she said, smiling. "Always foolin'. Don't let them bother you." She stopped at the door, found the right key among the many on her giant key ring, and we emerged with relief into the different atmosphere of the autistic unit. It was dim, empty, and quiet. "Georgie be down the hall," she said in dismissal, pointing me in the right direction. In a large room at the end of the wide corridor I saw Georgie, sitting at a table, playing with a puzzle. Although she was like a rag doll when I hugged her, offering neither resistance nor response, I felt that somehow she knew who I was. I sat down beside her on a little chair like hers and handed her a puzzle piece. She took it, and deftly put it in place. It was hard to believe she was retarded in the face of precocity like this, she was so nimble and quick when it came to puzzles, as well as tying shoes, getting dressed, cooking, and of course, drawing.

A soft-spoken, gentle woman in her fifties with fading strawberry blond hair and a placid face came and sat down with us. She introduced herself and said she was an occupational therapist. "Georgie's doing well, we're very encouraged," she said. "We're working closely with her and she's beginning to speak. You can work with her at home. She really seems to be quite a good little responder. She's determined." This conversation was the first positive one I'd ever had about Georgie and not only was she talking, but she was determined as well. This was something about her character, independent of her autism: this was her true spirit coming through. Finally we were heading in the right direction and I had a clear-cut idea of something I could do: Georgie and I could talk. I could get to know her now. It was the most exciting and wonderful prospect, not only for her sake but for my own. I hadn't realized until then how starved I'd been for information about her. Now I could find out what she was like, and how she felt. She didn't have to remain an enigma forever, and with speech there was hope that she would one day "function within the normal range," no matter what the doctors said her chances were.

Dr. Magda Campbell, the head of the unit, came over to the table to say hello. Her fine, shining dark hair was stretched into a perfect chignon and her smile was a therapeutic tool of warmth and brilliance. "We are so pleased with Georgie's adjustment," she said, her Hungarian accent coloring her words. "I hope you will have a pleasant weekend with her." The other psychiatrist on the service joined us, a mellow and relaxed woman who projected a calm intelligence which informed everything she said and did. She introduced herself, asked how I was, and left quickly with Dr. Campbell, leaving me stranded with a thousand questions that would have to wait until another time.

Georgie and I collected ourselves and her toothbrush, bathrobe, slippers, and hairbrush, and walked down the corridor, Georgie refusing my hand as usual. We passed Maria, the butt of the doctor's joke, sitting at a table, her arms moving like a marionette's, tilting up and waving aimlessly. Her head wobbled at an angle on her neck, her huge eyes glistening but vacant under oddly raised eyebrows.

Another child was with her, Emily, who was three, a year younger than Georgie. Emily was industriously working with plastic cubes, fitting them into the right places, her head down and her gestures careful and delicate. Her thin brown hair, waxen features, and the pale patch of color in her cheeks made her look like an old-fashioned doll. I stood for a moment in the doorway and she looked up at me and gave me not only a glance but a faint smile. She was far more advanced than Georgie.

At the back of the room, overseeing the children, sat a slightly disheveled woman who was smiling pleasantly. I caught a whiff of alcohol fumes as I passed her. When we were joined by Miss Dials, who would escort us to the elevator, I asked about her. "Oh, she's been here a long time. She's good with the kids. No one can reach them like she can. Don't worry about it." Although I cautioned myself to suspend judgment, not wanting to fall into the trap of being overly sober and critical, it bothered me.

In one of the bedrooms on the right I saw a large, looming figure shaking out a sheet. She glowered in our direction and went back to work. "I suppose she's good with the children, too," I said, hoping it was true. Miss Dials said she was.

In the corner of the hall near the door stood another little patient, dragging one toe and looking up at us beguilingly. He was three also, a tiny boy with close-cropped hair and a big grin. As Miss Dials found the key, he moved to follow us.

"Now you wait here, José," she said. "Nobody's going any-where except Georgie and her mother. Your mother not here yet." He sidled back toward me and looked up at me ingratiatingly.

"Good-bye, José," I said.

"Good-bye, José," he said softly. I looked questioningly at Miss Dials.

"Oh, that's echo speech," she said. "Echolalia. He repeats after you. They all do that sometimes if they talk." I thought of Georgie and her perfect imitation of the seals in Central Park. Was that echolalia, too?

Georgie and I walked to the corner of First Avenue and found a taxi. As we traveled the familiar FDR Drive to the Brooklyn Bridge, Georgie quietly gazed at her fingers, holding them up to the window. It started to rain, little drops sliding fitfully across the glass, and she watched their patterns as they combined and disintegrated in the wind. Never had a child been so easily entertained: boredom was an unknown state for her. I enjoyed myself too, in my own way, savoring the luxury of the cab ride and reveling in the news of Georgie's talking, and the fact that I was told she was determined, and a good responder to therapy. Knowing she was making progress made it so much easier to deal with the actuality of her being in "inpatient residential treatment," just like the little boy on "Marcus Welby, M.D." two years ago, when I'd thought it could never happen to Georgie and to me.

Her progress, and the fact that she was no longer deteriorating, reinforced my recently acquired belief that someone was watching over me now full-time, not just once in a while. As we moved through the traffic, I flashed back to an event that had radically altered my outlook. It had given me a sense of protection and guidance that thrilled and amazed me, and had stayed with me, changing my perspective and my perception of reality. It seemed that good could be extracted even from the bad things that were happening because the hundred-and-eighty-degree turn in my thinking had come about as a direct result of my intractable, miserable insomnia.

After throwing away my pills and swearing off alcohol, I began to have so much trouble sleeping that I felt as if I hadn't slept for three weeks. It was explained to me in my recovery group meetings that tranquilizers and alcohol had done so much damage to my nervous system that I might have insomnia for months.

I was advised to pray, and when I said I was an agnostic and didn't know whom to pray to, someone said, "Well then pray to whom it may concern. But *pray*."

I was embarrassed and skeptical, but decided to try it. What did I have to lose, I reasoned; it probably wouldn't work anyway. The fact that I needed such intervention offended my sense of autonomy and self-reliance but I had to admit I was desperate. I'd been hearing so much about "turning it over to a higher power" from people who seemed to be at peace with themselves, which I was not, that I'd decided it was only sensible to pay attention and follow their advice.

One night, I sat on my bed looking out at Pierrepont Street, lined with trees and stretching down to the harbor, the water reflecting the lights of the skyscrapers in the distance. Off in the sky, high up and far away, I pictured an attenuated figure in a long white robe on a cloud, the authoritarian God of my childhood, and feeling both ridiculous and sensible, I prayed to Him, asking His advice on a minor problem to do with Dotsie. My yearning for a cure for sleeplessness was only subliminally expressed. This small gesture of faith and relinquishment changed my life when I distinctly felt I got an answer "not from me," as the testimonials say. "You mean the man on the cloud talked back?" Dotsie asked when I told her about the experience.

"Yes, in a way He did," I said. "He spoke to my heart from His heart." She accepted it with the perfect faith of children, as if to say "why not?"

This "guidance" offered a solution I hadn't thought of to whatever small dilemma I'd turned over concerning Dotsie. But I could recognize that the answer was right, and that it seemed to have come when I prayed. I could give credit where credit was due. And now, to my amazement, although it was only eleven o'clock at night, I felt sleepy.

I hadn't remembered turning it on, but suddenly I noticed that beautiful music was coming from the radio, and as I sat on my bed listening, it seemed to swell, filling the room. It was unlike anything I'd ever heard before. After a few minutes, overwhelmed by my need to sleep, I crossed the room to turn off the radio, only to discover that it was *off*. As the music began to fade, I floated to my bed and drifted off to sleep in a daze.

The next morning I called a friend who was an expert on matters spiritual and psychological.

"What'd it sound like?" she asked.

"Impossible to describe," I said, "but celestial music with a gospel beat is as close as I can come. And it swelled in volume, it filled the room, and then it faded. And the radio was off the whole time. I checked and double-checked. The knob was at 'off.'"

"It was either an auditory hallucination due to coming off pills, or it was an authentic spiritual experience, I don't know which. And I've never heard of gradations in volume in an auditory hallucination."

"I don't know whether to identify with Joan of Arc or Ophelia," I said. She reassured me and told me not to worry about it, that in the beginning of a conversion experience, anything was possible. She'd heard similar stories although people were always reluctant to disclose them for fear of being thought of as nuts, or because skepticism and/or ridicule was hard to take. She said I should just store it away in a corner of my psyche as a wonderful mystery.

I waffled back and forth but finally admitted that it must have been a miracle, because the result was a complete healing of my insomnia and an infusion of faith that permanently altered my outlook.

Miracles in my personal life sustained me from then on, and I talked about them relentlessly and unabashedly to anyone who would listen. My more secular friends made disparaging remarks, thinking I'd made a lateral move from despondency to religious mania. I didn't care what they thought because I knew I was getting well, and it was a great feeling.

The impact on my life at home was wonderful. I began to change from negative to positive, life took on an orderly cast, and there was peace in my house. The vibes changed. In an urge for simplicity, I had the entire apartment painted white and threw out or gave away everything extraneous. I still never played the guitar around

Georgie, but now that she was away during the week, Dotsie and I began to sing inspirational popular songs with the guitar as accompaniment. We learned the words of "Bridge over Troubled Water," "Raindrops Keep Fallin' on My Head," and "Let It Be." "Let It Be" became our favorite: ". . . whispering words of wisdom, let it be." I had a copy of a hymnal, and although it sounded strange to sing hymns to the guitar, I thought, why not, and we sang current favorites as well as the ones I'd learned in my childhood. Now that I believed all of them, the words had new meaning, and they comforted me. If this was the opiate of the masses, it was powerful stuff, but it didn't feel like a drug. It felt like reality. It was just a reality I'd never known before. It was making it possible for me to act like the woman my uncle had told me about, the one who would smile when she said good morning no matter what.

I loved our apartment house, and felt that our solid, sunny rent-controlled apartment with its view of the water was the blessing of a lifetime. Our neighbors throughout the building were friendly, helpful, and supportive. I came to rely on them more and more. Kitty and Claire Griffin, two elderly sisters, lived next door. Kitty, who had assumed the role of Dotsie's surrogate grandmother, had invited Dotsie over while I went to pick up Georgie for the weekend from Bellevue. As Georgie and I stepped out of the elevator, they were waiting for us at the door.

"We heard the elevator and Kitty said it would probably be you," Dotsie said, smiling her new six-year-old smile with two teeth missing in the front. Kitty stood with her hand on Dotsie's shoulder.

"Now Dotsie," she said. "You go home and come back later when you've had supper and do some more of that play you were doing." I opened the door, letting both girls into the apartment, and Kitty said to me in a conspiratorial whisper, her carefully curled white hair glowing in the light from the stairwell, "Oh that Dotsie. She's the most entertaining little thing." Her thin, lined face lit up as she talked animatedly. "I'm just bowled over by her. She makes up the most wonderful plays and stories and songs, and she performs in so many different accents. I just love to listen to her." With the girls out of earshot, she suddenly grasped my arm as her eyes filled with tears. "I just can't believe it, I just can't believe it," she said. She ducked away, taking a handkerchief from her pocket as she shut her door quietly behind her.

Although it was a tremendous blessing that Kitty loved seeing so much of Dotsie, I was pulled up short by her grief. Her acceptance of leukemia as absolutely terminal was only logical, but nevertheless it was impossible for me. I wasn't ready to give up. And yet trying to avoid the reality also had its problems. The roller coaster of Dotsie's remissions, while unquestionably worth it, was a hard ride.

As I shrugged off my raincoat and hung it in the closet, I savored the feeling of being home, of being able to enter my haven, my own place, and relax. No man to cook for, nobody's hoops to jump through, nobody to tell me what to do. I felt like an indentured servant who had served my time and was now free.

I couldn't wait to start my first real conversation with Georgie, but wanted to make sure I didn't scare her away by making her feel pressured. I got some paper from the stack on the shelf and we all lay down on the floor on our stomachs to draw, something I had never done before. I drew two big boxes, one yellow and one red. "Which color do you like better, Georgie, red or yellow?" I asked, pointing to the boxes.

"Red or lellow," she said.

"No, which one do you like better, red or yellow?" Georgie didn't look at me but she appeared to be considering the question and preparing an answer which wasn't going to be a repetition.

"Red!" It was our first true verbal interaction, and I would never forget it. I wanted to dip it in bronze and put it on the mantelpiece.

"Georgie, which color do you like better, red or blue?"

"Blue."

"Okay, now which color do you like better, blue or green?"

"Gween."

"Which color do you like better, red or green?"

"Gween."

"Which color do you like better, yellow or green?"

"Gween!" I concluded from this conversation that green was Georgie's favorite color, an exciting and marvelous discovery. As mine was blue, her choice of green was hers alone. She could own it as an expression of her integrity.

One of the things we liked to do in the summer was to go out walking in the rain. Georgie didn't like using an umbrella for some reason, but Dotsie loved hers, and we would all go out in slickers and rubber flip-flops and slosh through the puddles. The ones with multicolored oil slicks we avoided, but they fascinated Georgie, who would squat down and stare until hauled away. Georgie was never as eager as Dotsie when I suggested a rain walk, but Dotsie and I loved them, from the glistening sidewalks to the peculiar light in the sky. We never went out when there was thunder or lightning, only when it was safe, and I couldn't figure out why we were always the only ones out there for pleasure. It seemed like a wonderful way to have fun while cooling off.

"What do you like better, sunshine or rain?" I asked Georgie.

"Sunsine."

"Do you like to go out in the rain?"

"Rain."

"No, Georgie, answer me yes or no. Do you like to go out in the rain? Answer me yes or no." Silence.

"No, you say yes and I'll give you a cookie."

"Cookie." I gave her the cookie. I couldn't resist.

"Now do you like to go out in the rain? Answer yes or no." Silence, as she munched on the cookie. I wasn't about to take the cookie away. Was this why she needed a neutral setting and a whole team of miracle workers with the distance and patience of Annie Sullivan? I rose to my knees and pulled her up for a bear hug, ignoring the fact that her arms hung at her sides and her head turned away. "I want a heart-to-heart hug," I said, celebrating how good I felt. I'd learned that heart-to-heart hugs came in handy at other times, too, when I was feeling unbearably sad and the contact would actually reduce the pain to a level I could stand. Dotsie, who was drawing a few feet away, got up, came over, and threw her arms around me, hugging exactly heart to heart. She pressed her cheek against mine, her fuzzy head brushing against my hair. "I love you, Mommy."

In the fall, Dotsie went on a new drug which seemed to work wonders, putting her into a remission which no one had expected. Since her white count was too high for school but she felt well, we had a whole winter of *carpe diem*, going all over New York together on excursions and adventures. When a friend of mine who'd grown up with my former father-in-law criticized him for neglecting his grandchildren, he bought me a car. It was used, but only two years old and in perfect condition. I hadn't seen him for over a year, and when he delivered it to me, he chuckled and said, "Gee, Annabel, you've got more problems than a dog has fleas." Oh well, at least I had my car, and I was grateful. Dotsie and I tootled around in it happily, playing the radio for all our favorite songs, creating special memories.

Just when I was beginning to accept and enjoy life, staying in the moment, and living a day at a time, I met someone who preached and practiced Christian Science. She believed that Dotsie's current remission was a permanent healing and had nothing to do with the drug she was on. I thought she might be right since the people at Sloan-Kettering said the drug had never achieved anything like the result Dotsie was experiencing. She informed me that the prevailing thinking in Christian Science was that doctors got in the way of God's healing power, that even their negative thought got in the way. She said my children's illnesses were illusions caused by my fears, and that if I could *know* they were God's perfect children, they would recover. The idea was that they were meant to be as well now as they would be in the afterlife, and that if I prayed and studied Mary Baker Eddy's *Key to the Scriptures*, did my Bible study, consulted a practitioner, went to a Christian Science church twice a week, and believed in mind over matter, my children would be healed. Although my guilt—engendered by believing I'd created my children's illnesses out of my own sick fear—was horrendous, especially when I thought I'd been moving away from irrational blame, the thought of having a formula for healing was still so seductive that I began to do everything my Christian Science friend told me to do. I was gung ho, never dreaming that finding Christian Science was like being given fresh horses in the middle of a battle and then finding out they were lame.

The first disillusionment occurred when I tried taking Georgie to Christian Science Sunday school, thinking if the teacher could "see Georgie well," she wouldn't manifest any symptoms. If Christian Science, and Bettelheim, for that matter, were right, then I had "enabled" Georgie to be autistic through robbing her of her autonomy, hovering over her, anticipating her needs, preventing her from maturing in the normal way. It was like the joke about the autistic boy in the shower. He's four years old, and has never said a word, when suddenly he calls, "Mommy, Mommy, the water's too hot!" His mother comes running: "Oh, my son! You spoke! How wonderful!" she says. He explains, "Well, up until now, everything was all right."

Because I had been terrified of retardation and brain damage because of the anoxia Georgie had suffered at birth, because she was so small, because I hadn't eaten properly in the first trimester, because I'd had second thoughts about wanting her, I was willing to try to believe that perhaps the fear of that alone had arrested Georgie's development, stopping her cold in her maturation processes. I had jinxed her, I had made her emotionally accident-prone in my entrenched belief that she was brain damaged, and had enabled her to act like a brain-damaged child when in fact, as I'd been so forcefully informed by the doctor at Rusk Institute, and Bruno Bettelheim, she was not. And if I'd enabled her in these destructive ways, I could change, get out of the way, allow God to work, and she would be healed. Convoluted thinking but understandable given the influences, the circumstances, and the degree of my grief and desperation.

As a foil to my self-pity, I'd been thinking about a Vietnamese mother I'd read about who had seen her family killed in a village raid, and had found the strength to go on. This Christian Science was a better way, I thought: I didn't have to lose my family after all, and everything was going to be all right. There was a long-established, respected religion which told me so, and this great God I'd so recently and dramatically discovered was in charge of it all.

When I picked Georgie up at Christian Science Sunday school, the teacher was shaking her head. "I had to do an awful lot of *knowing*," she said, exasperated, and my heart sank. It had been better in her old, conventional Sunday school, where they hadn't expected so much of her. They, at least, had welcomed her, and had never complained.

Dotsie continued to give me hope by doing unexpectedly beautifully on her drug. Georgie was progressing wonderfully at Bellevue and was changing and growing every day. She had stopped spinning, warbling, and barking like a seal, and her rocking had diminished. The program at Bellevue was so structured that there was little free time, and she was consistently reprimanded for any self-stimulating behavior.

The children played, worked, and had their meals in a large, sunny, uncluttered room where things such as blocks, puzzles, and beads were neatly kept in closed, locked cupboards. Compared to Georgie's nursery school last year, with its welter of toys, books, easels, blackboards, muscial instruments, and noisy interacting children, the atmosphere at Bellevue was as quiet as a tomb.

In this atmosphere Georgie stopped deteriorating and began to grow. She was able to learn. And coincidentally, I had mirrored her behavior at home, or was it the other way around? I had stopped deteriorating, and had begun to grow. My reaction to autism, leukemia, and divorce had peaked, and I was learning how to take care of myself, be responsible, and make the best of it. Although the pain of it all was still horrendous, Georgie must have been able to sense and draw from the peace which was at the center of my life.

Speech was taught daily at Bellevue through the use of a felt board and brightly colored felt objects. "What is this?" the occupational therapist would say to the nine preschoolers sitting on little yellow chairs. Some were able to watch, and some couldn't focus their eyes. "Is this a house?" She would hold up a soft, fuzzy, and vibrantly colored house. "Georgie, what is this? Say 'house.' "

"House," Georgie would say. As a reward, she would be allowed to hold the letter before it was put on the board.

If Christian Science could be believed, Georgie would be able to continue on her upswing and improvement whether she was at Bellevue or not because a divine process was at work.

I thought of trying to share these feelings in the weekly group-therapy sessions I attended for mothers at Bellevue, but I thought better of it. "For those who understand, no explanation is necessary; for those who don't, no explanation is possible." If "letting go of fear" and "seeing them well" were the linchpins of my children's recoveries, how could I expect the therapist who ran the meetings to understand? Miss Wile was a pragmatic, analytical social worker. She was also a warm, appealing woman with a wry sense of humor who did her utmost to convince the mothers—all guilt-ridden to some degree—that autism's genetic and constitutional factors were all-important, and that we were not to blame. "You did your best," she would say. She said that people help and hinder in terms of environment in dealing with any illness or handicap, some more than others, and that how the children were treated by us was important. But autism was still officially labeled "etiology unknown." When I said Bettelheim would disagree, she said that Bettelheim didn't know everything, only spouted theories, and had no proof. I would go home from group therapy mulling this over and deciding I wasn't a monster after all. Then the Christian Scientists would tell me that autism was my own invention. I swung between the two like a tether ball.

I'm sure I wouldn't have embraced Christian Science if I hadn't been nursing monumental guilt. In some ways I think I needed to believe that my children's illnesses were my fault, and that if I changed enough, they would recover. It gave me a feeling of control, a defense against my helplessness. I had a nightmare where I was in a vast, brown, dimly lit courtroom being accused of neglecting Georgie and causing her to go out of her mind. I was crying, admitting that I should have loved her more, hugged her more, stimulated her more, and somehow managed to be a better mother, and I knew I was guilty. I woke up just before I was to be sentenced (probably to death by hanging).

I seemed to need to put on a hair shirt, at least for now.

At Memorial there was general rejoicing over Dotsie's unexpected remission although I was cautioned not to get my hopes up too high since it couldn't last. Since she'd already lived six months longer than they said she would, I thought they were being unnecessarily pessimistic and short-sighted. How did they really know anyway? According to one of the nurses, who had made a point of telling me, spontaneous, permanent, unexpected remissions happened at Memorial once in a while. I hung on to the belief that we would be in that small, favored minority, and that these halcyon days would go on forever.

When we'd moved to our new apartment and had become friends with Tom and Doris, our 'cross-the-hall neighbors, Dotsie and their daughter Evie became best friends. Dotsie played in their apartment often, and I was glad she had their example of a normal family life with both parents present. They were warm and loving, and treated her as one of their own. Tom told me that once, when he yelled at the girls for jumping on the bed, Dotsie's comment was "Oh! God save me from this man!" The neighbors on my floor became like our extended family.

We had an open door policy, and Evie and Dotsie were back and forth constantly, lugging plastic suitcases bulging with Barbie doll clothes, rigging their Barbies out by the hour for every activity imaginable. On the weekends, Evie's sister Louisa, who was two, would come over to "play" with Georgie. They would sit three or four feet apart on the floor and scribble and draw. They didn't interact, but at least they weren't alone, and I kept hoping they would start talking to each other because Georgie was becoming more reachable in subtle ways. It was becoming easier to divert her from her autistic behavior, and she began to be able to respond to discipline. Her spinning and warbling stopped, and she spent less time gazing at her fingers. She had occasionally walked on her toes, an odd, inexplicable manifestation of the disorder, and this she stopped doing completely. She was able to phase out her habit of allowing her tongue to loll on her lower lip while breathing with her mouth open. She never initiated a conversation, still preferring to pull me by my clothes toward anything she wanted help with, such as getting a cookie or a glass of milk. But when I asked her to say "cookie" or "milk," she would, and would have a certain guarded but definite look of satisfaction on her face for having said the word. She still made no eye contact, and even when bribed with the most luscious of treats, her eyes seemed milky and unfocused when she tried to look at me. But at least she tried.

Some of her behavior was completely baffling. On the trip to Bellevue she would often be difficult, reacting in incomprehensible ways. Once, when I discovered a new way onto the Brooklyn Bridge, a shortcut which involved driving past the St. George Hotel, Georgie suddenly crouched down in the back seat with her hands over her ears. She moaned and rocked back and forth on the seat with her eyes shut and then began to scream in a high-pitched wail.

"What is it, Georgie?" I asked, pulling over.

"Dat! Dat!" She took one hand off an ear just long enough to point in the direction of the hotel. All I could see was an unbroken expanse of beige brick, uninterrupted by windows on the bottom ten floors. Only a hole in the wall was visible, three feet from the sidewalk and six inches in diameter.

"I can't hear anything," I said. While Georgie remained cowering on the back seat, wailing, Dotsie and I went over to the hole in the wall to investigate. It was covered with thick wire mesh and an intermittent puffing sound was coming from it. We went back to the car. I got into the back seat and pulled Georgie on my lap, taking her hands off her ears and holding them.

"It's making a puffing noise, Georgie. Is that what you don't like?" She wrenched her hands away and slammed them back over her ears, throwing herself onto the car seat with her head burrowing in the corner.

"Okay," I said. "Then we won't go near it again." I moved into the driver's seat and turned the corner. Even after we were a block away, Georgie was still in her position of retreat. When I yelled, "Can you still hear it?" she gingerly unhooked a hand. Evidently she couldn't, and she relaxed, and proceeded to undulate her fingers and stare at them, content again. It was hard to prevent her from this particular self-stimulating exercise in the car when there was no way of distracting her.

On the FDR Drive we drove along smoothly until we got to the construction site of an apartment complex that was being built out into the East River. Gigantic pile drivers were ramming huge round wooden piles into the river bottom, and the noise was ear-splitting even for Dotsie and me. As a detour wasn't possible, Dotsie jumped into the back seat in anticipation, and clamped her arms around Georgie's already barricaded ears. Between the two of them we got through it.

These noises caused Georgie actual pain, and yet we never knew which ones would and which ones wouldn't. She could stand the subway and the bus didn't seem to faze her, and yet a puffing sound that was barely audible drove her to distraction. It made no sense.

In March, Georgie had been in the Bellevue program for eight months and had been jogged, I thought, into a recovery process that would continue regardless of whether she was at home all the time or at Bellevue. My Christian Scientist friend, who I thought was a clear-thinking, well-educated paragon of virtue, was disturbed about all the drugs Georgie was being given as part of the experimental research being done at Bellevue, and I was upset about them, too. She urged me to stop having her treated there. And so, on a bleak, windy day in March, I absconded with Georgie on a Friday night, packing her up and taking her home with no intention of returning her on Sunday. I thumbed my nose at the medical profession, and when Dr. Campbell called me and urged me to bring her back, I said I felt Georgie was well enough to be home and would be the better for it.

Two days later, Bill called to tell me he had lost his job. He was unemotional about it, saying he planned to pick up enough money by driving a cab to provide us with groceries and gasoline. Rent would be beyond him, at least for a while. As I was already driving an uninsured car, and sweeping the apartment with a broom because I couldn't afford to have the vacuum repaired, this new blow felt like the proverbial last straw. I didn't see how I could work myself when Georgie's future depended so much on my ability to meet her needs, and Dotsie was a full-time job as well. Fear of destitution and homelessness washed over me in a great wave. I told Bill I didn't think I could stand the insecurity. "Well, I guess we just shouldn't have had children," he said philosophically. I had gotten over the intense rage I'd felt toward him, and the homicidal fantasies I'd had when I'd drowned my sorrows in front of the television almost a year ago, but this comment made me feel a pervasive, helpless frustration that was almost as painful as the anger had been. I felt abandoned. His family could have helped us, I knew, but I guess they had simply refused. I was left holding the bag and it wasn't fair.

Resolutely, I "put faith in the place of fear," and turned the problem over. "You take it, I can't handle it," I prayed. I believed there would be a way to manage, that I couldn't see it yet, and that the solutions would come before it was too late.

Chapter 6

Coping

Georgie was "mainstreamed" into a tiny nursery school run by the city in a nearby park. I tried to imagine she'd be fine. The fact that denial rather than faith was at work was an idea I dismissed as negative thought. She played quietly in school in the corner for the rest of the spring, and the only problem I had with her was placating the teacher when she complained, not surprisingly, that Georgie was getting nothing out of the program.

I enrolled her in a modern dance class but the teacher's stricken face when I picked her up told me we wouldn't be back. Apparently the music had set Georgie off, and she had been relentless in her efforts to escape from the room. The teacher, who had forcibly restrained her for the entire hour as she fought to get away, was wild and sweating when I arrived. Glancing at each other from the corners of their eyes, the other mothers faded off as the teacher's breathing calmed to the point where she could give me her opinion. As if it were a revelation to her, she rolled her eyes and said, "This is not something that could be caused by the environment." Humiliated, baffled, and mystified as to why Georgie behaved the way she did, I took her home, holding her by the wrist when she wouldn't hold my hand.

In her behavior at home, Georgie didn't regress at all, and I was increasingly sure I had done the right (and noble and gutsy) thing. I was certain she had turned the corner, and that when the time came a year and a half from now, she would be ready to read and write in first grade. The fact that she wasn't able to grasp the concept or meaning of numbers or letters didn't worry me too much. She'd catch up as her general condition improved. The fact that she continually stroked people's hair at random, and wouldn't say yes, only no, concerned me, but I was sure she'd outgrow all that. I thought it was odd that she never used pronouns, and referred to herself as Georgie. And she still didn't play with anyone, but that was going to change. It upset me when she played so obsessively with her hoards of plastic cowboys and Indians. She lined them up by the hour in great sweeping curves and then laughingly mowed them all down in a row like dominoes, her eyes squinting in tense little crescents as if she needed to filter light in some way. But as long as her time spent on activities like this was harmless, what did it matter? So much of this she would simply outgrow eventually. Or so I told myself.

In the meantime, I applauded her for certain aspects of her self-sufficiency. She got herself dressed and undressed, chose her clothes, brushed her teeth and her hair, ate well, and slept well. The fact that she was virtually unteachable and disaffected, and picked up skills by osmosis, didn't seem so insurmountable. She would become more tractable with time. And she could learn to use her drawing ability to her advantage. Her pictures had become increasingly intricate and impressive although they were still nonrepresentational. And although she still didn't initiate conversations, she had begun speaking in short sentences. She was going to be fine.

A week after Georgie left the Bellevue program, Dotsie, who I had almost stopped worrying about, lost her remission. I was so profoundly surprised and disappointed I could barely function, and came close to caving in completely. I was sure it was my fault. I must have done something wrong, maybe the stress of taking Georgie out of Bellevue was too much for Dotsie and me, had reawakened my fears, and had triggered the relapse. I prayed harder and went to Christian Science meetings faithfully but Dotsie was very sick. She and Georgie both came down with mumps, and mumps for Dotsie was life-threatening. She got pneumonia for the fourth time, and by the time she had recovered, she was emaciated. It was hard to believe that two months ago we had been enjoying our delightful excursions. We had even managed to see Dotsie's favorite musical, *Man of La Mancha*, twice, at matinees.

Since I had been told by my Christian Science mentor that the drugs at Sloan-Kettering were blocking her recovery, I was in a quandary. I was so tired of getting my hopes up and then having them dashed, never knowing whether she would live or die, that I think I was willing to gamble everything on anything. This included the possibility of taking her off all drugs, avoiding in the process the harmful side effects, the ulceration, the nausea, and the depression of her immune system.

At the Christian Science meeting the next Wednesday, I heard a man testify to having been healed of terminal cancer by refusing all drugs and medical treatment and believing God would heal him. And a fellow parishioner called to tell me that finally, after reading thousands of testimonials, she had found a witness to a healing of leukemia through Christian Science in California. That did it. I decided I had to try it; I would never forgive myself if I didn't. The next day Dotsie was very sick when she woke up, and normally I would have taken her to the hospital. But I took care of her at home instead, reading to her, and giving her chicken broth, and desperately hoping that without drugs she would suddenly start to improve. That night a friend came over to keep the vigil with me, and as Dotsie's breathing became ragged as she slept, I panicked and dialed 911. A policeman came, and sympathetic to what we were trying to do, he brought an oxygen tank and stayed for an hour to talk and offer encouragement. All night long my friend and I prayed, believing and hoping against hope that we were right, that without medicine Dotsie would suddenly rally and begin a pure and total recovery, becoming, as the Christian Scientists predicted, God's perfect child.

In the morning she was near death and we were exhausted and defeated. We looked at each other hopelessly, and I said, "I'm calling an ambulance." Within five minutes we could hear the sirens blaring as it pulled up to the front door. Dotsie and I rushed to the hospital. Her heartbeat was faint, her hands were ice cold, and her hemoglobin was down to three, but she responded visibly to the transfusion she was given and the crisis passed. The people at Sloan-Kettering were understandably tight-lipped and distant when I brought Dotsie in, feeling I had been willfully and criminally negligent. I tended to agree with them but tried to explain that I was a fool rather than a criminal as I'd had the best of intentions. They just shook their heads even though they admitted that since they had used all their "best" drugs, there was now, from a medical standpoint, virtually no hope for her recovery.

My disillusionment in Christian Science was complete when a practitioner I knew well got cancer of the brain. He chose, to my amazement, that exercise in hypocrisy known as surgery, and actually appeared in public with his shaven, swollen head a symbol of failure. Then he died. Evidently no amount of faith, prayer, believing, knowing, Bible reading, or mind over matter had been able to help the practitioner, although there were thousands of bona fide healings recorded in Christian Scientist publications, and I thought they must be genuine.

The important thing, I concluded, was to live each day well, and to die a good death, regardless of when and how. For my own wonderful Dotsie I tried to accept the undeniable fact that her illness was described as terminal. The problem was that I couldn't bear to have her life cut short. It seemed totally unnatural, a terrible waste. But I would try to be reasonable now, believing that if, barring a miracle, the worst happened, both she and I would be given the strength when the time came.

As a result of my behavior, I was hauled on to the carpet at Sloan-Kettering, facing an inquisition headed up by the staff psychiatrist. I felt reckless, defensive, and humiliated by defeat as I faced him.

He was seated behind a large, empty desk, his face a mask of objective indifference. I remained standing, like a prisoner brought before the warden. "How do you feel about the deepest part of yourself?" he inquired, as if I were beneath contempt. I bristled at the implications.

"I have a few questions along those lines about the doctors here, as a matter of fact," I surprised myself by saying.

"You have questions about the doctors here?" A question for a question, his thin, slicked-back hair glistening in the overhead light. He looked pale and unhealthy, as if he lived underground. I decided to shift the blame, and launched into an attack I'd been wanting to unleash for months.

"I think it must take a special kind of doctor to work here. First they give you false, overly negative information about how long they think your child is going to live. Then they bombard the kids with experimental drugs and use them as guinea pigs. A lot of the procedures are painful and some of them are downright barbaric. One of the doctors told me he had been counseled to build as thick a shell as possible. He was criticized for showing compassion. For being human! How do you think the *doctors* feel about the deepest part of themselves, that's the question you should be asking. I came to Sloan-Kettering for the best care for my daughter and instead you give her drugs with horrible side effects and most of them don't work anyway. You don't even expect them to work. You can't blame me for trying something else. The hematologist at Brooklyn Hospital warned me not to come here, she knew it was demoralizing and depressing. I wish I'd listened to her. Oh, and in answer to your question, I *like* the deepest part of myself, thank you, and I've fought hard for my daughter's life."

"Yes, well, that's very good." He cleared his throat and stood up to signal the end of our session. I said good-bye and left, feeling proud of myself, and went down to the donor room to give platelets. Platelets, which Dotsie often needed, are the clotting factor in the blood. In a healthy person they are regenerated quickly, and can be given three times a week. Whole blood is taken, the platelets are extracted from it, and the red cells are returned to the donor. Like many of the parents at Memorial, I was a habitué of the donor room, and appreciated the relaxing and fun atmosphere the two zany nurses in charge managed to create. They made the donor room an oasis, a place to go for a laugh and a sympathetic ear.

Georgie finished out the year at nursery school, coming with me to Memorial in the afternoons if Dotsie needed treatment or was an inpatient. I worried about the effect of the hospital on Georgie although she never seemed to react to anything there. I knew that nobody, no matter how heavily defended, could have gone through the experience of Sloan-Kettering unscathed. I used to equate entering the waiting rooms with crossing the River Styx, especially if adults with disfiguring malignancies were in evidence. I would picture my friends walking around nonchalantly outside, living their lives, unaware of the hell of the hospital with its dying patients, cool doctors, and endless, windowless treatment rooms. So when Occu (she was German, and her name sounded like Aku), my first-floor neighbor, offered to take Georgie when I went to the hospital, I accepted with relief.

Occu was a nursery school teacher with a daughter just Georgie's age. She said Georgie would just blend in with her children and do what they were doing, and would be no trouble. I began to drop Georgie off regularly, and even when it was every day for a while, Occu never complained or said it was inconvenient. And she would encourage me. Once she said, "You are fighting for your daughter's life and I admire you for it."

I didn't have the time or the energy for much of a social life beyond my group meetings and church. But I had met someone I'd been hoping to hold in reserve until my life became more manageable. When a friend invited me to a party in the very town where he just happened to live, it seemed only sensible that I invite him to escort me. When I called him, and he accepted, he asked me to have dinner with him. He said he couldn't wait until the party to see me. I couldn't resist, although I didn't have enough emotional energy left to imagine that anything would come of it.

His name was Peter, and when he came to pick me up at six o'clock, he walked in and greeted everyone warmly without a hint of discomfort or surprise. He looked appealing, handsome, and re-assuring in his Brooks Brothers suit as he walked over to the living room window and looked out.

"I can see my office," he said as he gazed toward an office building opposite us which fronted on the East River near Wall Street. His voice, which was as resonant as a radio announcer's, was filled with awe at this, as if he wished he could commute by cable car from my window to his. He looked over his shoulder at me and said, "I'd marry you for your apartment."

"You should be so lucky," I retorted, but I was pleased. We said good night to the children and the baby-sitter, and I felt like prancing when we were on the street walking to his car. It felt so good to be out. He wanted to stop off at his sister's apartment in Manhattan for a drink as it was her birthday, and I flattened my back against the seat as we whisked up the FDR Drive in fifteen minutes. When he came within a hair's breadth of a car he was passing, I gasped, and he glanced at me.

"Don't worry," he said. "I flew jets in the Air Force for three years in formation, and I learned not to hit things." I decided to relax and let the man drive, but it was difficult. It took an act of will and a leap of faith, but as we sped on, I had to admit he was good.

Soon we were sitting on a terrace looking south over the city, enjoying the clear June night and sipping Perrier with his sister and her husband. I realized she had been the assistant buyer in the college shop at Bloomingdale's when I'd worked there one summer, and it seemed like an amazing coincidence. We spent an hour with her and her husband, catching up, celebrating her birthday, and playing with their two tiny children. It seemed so civilized, healthy, and normal compared to my life.

We went to a romantic restaurant with a garden and a waterfall. With the wind rustling in the trees and the stars twinkling, and delicious food in front of us, we virtually interviewed each other. With expanding awe, as we covered all the ground we could think of, we realized how much we had in common—background, values, tastes, even the fact that our grandfathers had been in the same business seemed significant. We had both been through agony over our divorces and had come out the other side. Most important, we had both had "midlife conversion experiences" which we'd had a hard time explaining to most of our old friends, and which we were relieved and delighted to be able to talk about together. Even when he told me he was being transferred to Switzerland in two weeks, the idea that our relationship was meant to be grew in his mind and mine until, by the end of the evening, we were convinced we were Mr. and Mrs. Right. As I looked at him sitting there at the table under the trees, with the white sound of the waterfall splashing in the background, he looked happy and relaxed and ready to take on anything. I felt as if I'd been expecting him.

The next day, June 10, 1970, was my thirty-first birthday, but as Dotsie woke up with a high fever, any celebration would have to wait. I dropped Georgie off at Occu's, and Dotsie and I drove up to Memorial. She would probably have to be admitted, and that would mean another week or two of IVs and medicine. She was a good sport about it as always and settled in happily with her television set after saying hello to the nurses and the kids she knew.

That afternoon when I drove home, I felt drained as I always did when I left Dotsie at the hospital overnight, even though her roommate was someone she knew well. The day was clear and sunny, and the promenade and Victorian brownstones of Brooklyn Heights looked charming and inviting in the distance, like a dramatization of an Edith Wharton novel. I expected to park the car, pick up Georgie, and have a quiet evening at home. The night before seemed almost like a dream. I had thought about Peter all day but didn't dare try to grasp any implications or believe he would call me as he'd said he would.

I pulled into my street, and Occu, who had been watching for me, left the curb and began to walk down the middle of the street toward my car. She had a huge grin on her face, and she was carrying a shiny white box almost as big as she was. People in our building were looking out their windows in the brilliant sunlight, and Georgie was sitting on the front steps with Occu's children. I pulled up to the curb and jumped out of the car, feeling like a child on Christmas. There was no traffic to spoil the moment as I opened the box and saw the dozen yellow roses, with the card inside that said, "Happy Birthday. I love you, Peter." My eyes filled with tears as I hugged Occu. He was going to see me through, and even though it seemed too good to be true, I knew it was.

Our feelings were confirmed the next time we saw each other, and we took it on faith that his moving to Lausanne wouldn't be an insurmountable obstacle. After all, since we both spoke French and loved Europe, we'd be naturals together as expatriates, and we could find a way to have my children treated over there. Lausanne, with its picturesque houses sandwiched between the Alps and the Jura Mountains on Lake Geneva, sounded as romantic to me as a South Sea island, and with love, we reasoned, anything was possible.

During the time he had left, we saw each other as much as we could without neglecting Dotsie and Georgie. When I brought him to meet Dotsie in the hospital, they had instant and phenomenal rapport, and acted like old pals. I got the feeling that she liked seeing us together, that it made her feel secure.

Peter took Georgie in stride, accepting her as the quiet, extremely good (as long as you didn't try to get her to do something she didn't want to do) little girl that she was, complimenting me on how well she had learned to say "please" and "thank you" and how she never had to be entertained. He didn't know much about autism and took my word for it when I told him about how much progress she had made and how I thought she would be able to continue to go to a normal school.

Peter had been divorced for two years and had three children, who were thirteen, eleven, and nine. Although he worried about leaving them, he planned to have them visit, and he would see them every six weeks when he returned to the States on business. Since the divorce, they had stayed with him on alternate weekends in the little place he had rented near theirs, spending the rest of their time with their mother. When I met them, I loved the fact that they were healthy, normal kids. They were appealing and affectionate and obviously crazy about their father. He did have a wonderful way with them, and I wasn't surprised to learn that he had the honor of having six godchildren.

On the one Saturday we had together before Peter left, I drove out to Long Island with Georgie to the beach club he belonged to. We met Peter and his family by the pool. "Look over there on the high dive," he said. And there was Pam, his eldest daughter, tall and blond like her father, concentrating as she readied herself against the bright blue sky for a perfect swan dive. As we stood and watched in admiration, Kitty, his petite and wiry eleven-year-old, came up, said hello, and grabbed him by the arm. "Come on, Daddy, you *know* you want to go in." Hunt, who was nine, ran up to help her in the mighty struggle, and Peter finally gave in. He created such a crater as he hit that waves sloshed over the children's toes as they laughed and applauded on the sidelines.

Kitty and Pam baby-sat for Georgie, taking her gently into the water and playing with her in the shallow end. Georgie edged along the sides of the pool, splashing delightedly and kicking her feet. They thought she was so cute, they said, but very shy (she wouldn't look at them). When Peter told them she was autistic, it didn't seem to make much of an impression on them. I sat there taking it all in in the bright sunshine, wishing it could last forever.

Peter's parents had died of cancer in their fifties, and we'd just seen his sister, who was his only sibling, so the only family remaining to be met was my own. My brothers and my mother liked him, as I knew they would, and only hoped, although they never said so, of course, that he was as serious about me as he seemed. When his sister warned him that he was taking on a lot because of my children, he reassured her. "I can handle it," he said.

When he left for Switzerland and we said good-bye, I didn't

see how I could stand it. He said he would find a house big enough for us all, and that I would someday be able to join him. When the first of his letters arrived, I was beside myself with excitement, tearing open the envelope and whipping out the pages even before I got on the elevator. I could picture him sitting outside under the apple tree near the house he had found for us in the little village of Meis. It had three bedrooms and was gray stucco with a light green tiled roof, typical of the houses near Lausanne. In the photograph he sent me I could see billowy short white curtains in French windows framed by milky green wooden shutters. There was a little fenced-in garden full of roses, and the Jura Mountains rose up in the distance across the fields.

Although he hadn't formally proposed to me before he left, in July, when he'd been gone a month, he asked me to marry him. Taking time to think, I wrestled with the thought that it wasn't fair to saddle him with my problems. I wondered if I should believe him when he said that since he loved me, I was not taking advantage of him in any way. I felt like someone drowning who was worried about sinking the rescue craft, but when I tried to summon the faith that I'd be all right without him, I couldn't. So I said yes.

Chapter 7

The Quality of Life

several weeks later, Dotsie was still an inpatient, and when I went to see her one day, I got a surprise which taught me something about the quality of life. She was propped up in bed against several pillows, drawing on her hospital tray table, when I came in.

"Hi, sweetheart," I said, gingerly giving her a hug so as not to jar her IV. Even though it rested on a splint, and the needle was elaborately taped, the slightest sudden movement could be painful and could even dislodge it, causing it to infiltrate. If that happened, she would have to endure being hooked up again, and it had become difficult to find a vein.

"Hi, Mommy. See my playground scene?" I looked at the drawing. It was charming and full of detail, as were all her drawings, with appropriate expressions on the round faces of the children.

"Oh, look at that," I said. "You sure have everything in there —sandbox, slide, swings, jungle gum. The sprinkler's a great idea." A nurse appeared at the door.

"Hi, Dotsie. Is it ready?" She winked at me.

"I'm just finishing it." Dotsie signed it and held it up to be admired. "Like it?" She grinned proudly.

"Oh, it's wonderful," the nurse said. "I'm going to put it right up on my wall. How much did you say it was? I think you said a dollar." She rummaged in her pocket and pulled out a wrinkled dollar bill.

"Yes," Dotsie said, taking the money and handing her the picture. When her customer had left, Dotsie took a box from her bedside table and put it on the hospital tray in front of her. It was my old strong box, black and dented, which I had saved from childhood and had given to her. She lifted the lid and added the dollar to what I could see was a considerable stash. She looked at me sideways, and I asked her what was going on.

"Well, I have a sort of business," she said. "I sell my drawings." When I told her I was impressed and thought it was a great idea, she relaxed. "I know you don't like me to ask people for money, so I wasn't sure you would think it was okay to sell my pictures."

"I just don't like you to ask aunts and uncles and friends for money, that's all. But it's different when you give people something in return. That's the way the world works. How much money have you made?"

"Sixty-five dollars and forty cents." I tried to get used to the idea that not only was she a successful entrepreneur at the age of seven, but she'd done it completely on her own.

"I'm impressed. But where'd the forty cents come from? I thought the pictures cost a dollar, or fifty cents. Do you have some that are cheaper?"

"Yes," she said. "They start at five cents. I do a little scene on a sheet of writing paper, without coloring it, for a nickel. I do four different scenes, whichever one they want. I do a bigger one for a dime, on a regular piece of paper, and color it for a quarter. Then I do a big one on my best paper for fifty cents, and color it for a dollar. My sketch pad paper. Besides the playground one I do a bedtime scene, a taking-a-bath scene, and a birthday party. People come from all over the hospital, not just from where the kids are. I think a lot of people know about my business. I'm going to start a picture now, a dollar one, for Mr. Spielberg." She reached down to the foot of her bed and took her large sketch pad, opened it up, and began to work. "He wants a birthday party, with a lot of balloons in different colors."

"Well, you thought it up and did it all on your own. I'm so proud of you." I got up to go. "You really are something." I ruffled her little crew cut. "And I love your fuzzy head."

"I know," she said. "Everybody loves my fuzzy head."

Within two weeks, Dotsie's infection was under control and she was established on another drug. We settled down to weather July and August in Brooklyn Heights, spending hours outside in the playgrounds. Georgie loved sitting in the sprinkler in her bikini bottoms, and played endlessly in the jets of water which shot out in great arcs, cooling the rough concrete and making rainbows.

Toward the end of July, Peter's company decided to close the Lausanne office and send him home. Although my lovely hopes of Swiss living were dashed, I could see that it was for the best.

In late August, he flew in from Geneva, and when I drove to the airport to meet him, my anxiety levels were so high that I had trouble believing the car would hold together on the road. When we got back to Brooklyn Heights, I worried that grim reality was about to hit him full force and I was terrified. After all, if the children's father had run from us, how could I expect someone who barely knew them to cope? But Peter, being Peter, was fine. He explained for the tenth time that since he had fallen in love with me he accepted the entire package without hesitation.

By the end of August, he had three job offers which interested him, and we began to make plans to get married. We decided to elope and invited two couples who were close friends to come for the ceremony and for dinner afterward. My mother agreed to babysit for the weekend. We were sorry not to be able to include the children, his or mine, but there was no way I could manage to get married at all unless we kept it simple. We set the date for the first Friday in October.

Dotsie and Georgie were both going to the local public school, and although it was working out reasonably well, with both children actually in school at the same time sometimes, it was still the same old story. Dotsie was missing school half the time because she was sick, and Georgie "wasn't getting anything out of it." I thought if a teacher told me that one more time, I'd scream. It was hard to believe that they were already in second grade and kindergarten. I didn't want to think about Georgie in first grade. I knew there was no way she could learn to read and write in the usual fashion, but I took refuge in the belief that there would have to be some solution I hadn't thought of yet. She still made strange noises, had no eye contact, touched people's hair, and had no affect or expression of feelings. It was impossible to imagine her verbalizing normal human emotion, although she would occasionally say things like "Georgie hungry." If I asked her if she were sad, or happy, she would echo and say, "Georgie sad," or Georgie happy," with no ring of authenticity, as if she were performing a conversational exercise. If I said, "I love you," or "Georgie, Mommy loves you so so much," and hugged her and kissed her, she always shrugged and wiggled herself away and made no response, not even echo speech. If she had been on a desert island with only a stocked refrigerator and a landscape to enjoy, she would have been fine as long as we could have brought her a lifetime supply of groceries.

Peter's kids spent several days with us in September. They were wonderful with Dotsie and Georgie, and they sensed that it was important for me to have healthy, normal children in my life. I appreciated them, but still, there was so much for all of us to get used to. How in the world, I thought, could it all work out.

Although our wedding was simple, it was nonetheless a blessed occasion. Afterward, we drove to a restaurant on a river for a feast with our friends. Then we had the rest of the weekend to spend alone together for our minihoneymoon.

When Peter moved in, we became partners as parents, each trying to nurture our own and each other's children. It was hard, and without our faith, we never would have made it. As it was, we went to our group meetings, said our prayers, hung on to our positive thinking, and muddled through, learning and growing, and even laughing sometimes. I was trying very hard to be a good wife and mother and stepmother, putting up a brave front although I knew I hadn't properly faced Georgie's problem and was distraught over Dotsie's deteriorating condition. I had a lot to learn about communicating and trust, and should have believed Peter when he told me he would never, ever leave me no matter what.

Although my stepchildren appreciated certain things about me, like the fact that I allowed myself Bazooka bubble gum as a replacement for my cigarettes (and prided myself on the size of my bubbles), it was hard for them to adjust to their new family. It was then that Peter's enthusiasm would kick in, and his affirmations would keep me going. And luckily, we were never down at the same time.

Dotsie's eighth birthday was coming soon, and now that she was so desperately sick, I was afraid she'd have to celebrate it at the hospital. I talked to Miss Anderson about it, the nurse who had told me that people sometimes had spontaneous, permanent remissions that mystified the doctors. She said that parties were often given on the pediatric floor. Dotsie could be wheeled down to the playroom in her bed, if need be, and there would be balloons, and music, and a cake. It didn't sound so bad.

"There's something else we need to discuss," she said, and asked me to follow her down the hall to a small office where we could sit down together and have some privacy.

"You must talk to Dotsie," she said. She was normally cheerful, but now her expression was intense and serious. "She knows she has leukemia."

"No, she doesn't." I knew she didn't know because she would have told me. "I *know* she doesn't know. She has no idea. She thinks it's anemia. That's what she calls it."

"She *does* know," said Miss Anderson. "We're absolutely positive that she knows." She sounded as if she had the whole of Sloan-Kettering behind her.

"How can you be so sure?" I couldn't stand the thought of

Dotsie's reaction and couldn't believe that my elaborate charade of three years hadn't worked.

"Some of the other children have told us that Dotsie's talked about it with them. She knows you don't want her to know, and she's trying to protect you."

"What?" I was incredulous. "*She's* trying to protect *me?*" This was crazy. I wanted to run out of the room.

"She's trying to protect you from knowing that she knows. Believe me, it happens all the time around here. And it really isn't fair to her. You *have* to talk about it, she needs you, she needs your full support. She knows, for instance, that some of the children have died."

"How'd she find out?"

"Actually she figured it out when she didn't see them anymore and knew they were too sick to go home. Then she asked some of the other kids and they told her she was right, they had died." How awful it must have been for her.

"Does she know she's dying?" I asked, knowing what Miss Anderson was going to say but hoping that maybe I was wrong. It seemed I could be wrong about a lot.

"Yes," said Miss Anderson, with a terrible finality. "Please talk to her. She needs you."

Dotsie was sitting up in bed watching television when I came in to her room. Carla, her roommate, was there, along with her mother. I said hello to them although it had been hard for me to be polite to Carla's mother ever since the day she'd knocked a glass of juice out of Georgie's hand in the waiting room after Dotsie had taken a sip. "Don't you know she can get *sick* from that?" she'd yelled at me. I had reassured her, telling her it wasn't possible, but she had never believed me. The impasse had kept us from having a more supportive relationship.

"Dotsie," I said as I kissed her. "Let's go for a walk."

"Okay." She clambered out of bed on the far side, juggling her

IV like a pro. She took the pole in her right hand, wriggled her feet into her slippers, and started moving slowly around the end of the bed. We started down the corridor, passing the nurses' station on our left, and an emaciated boy who was in a bed against the wall.

"Hi, Tommy," Dotsie said as we went by, flashing him her smile with her newly symmetrical front teeth. They had come in perfectly.

"Hi." Tommy's cheeks were sunken, and his arms were as big around as shower poles. He was hooked up to an IV and rested on one elbow, watching everything that went on with huge, sad eyes. Dotsie waved to the nurses behind the tall counter and followed me into the little office Miss Anderson and I had been using.

"Why is Tommy out in the hall?" I asked.

"Because he got lonely in his room, and he's so sick the nurses want him near them."

"Dotsie." I went over to one of the chairs and sat down. "Come and sit with me." Dragging her pole behind her, she sat on my lap and leaned back against my shoulder. I hugged her and turned her so she could see me, thinking how hard it was to believe she was almost eight, and that she'd been sick for over three years. She'd been given only a year to live. A day at a time. We had packed a lot of quality time into the two extra years.

"Dotsie, do you remember Joey?" I named one of the children who had died.

"Sure."

"What happened to him?"

"He was too sick to go home." She looked at me expectantly.

"I know what happened to Joey," I said.

"You do?" She looked at me out of the corner of her eye.

"Yes, I do."

"The kids and I think he died."

"That's what I think too. He had cancer."

"I have it too. The anemia. It's cancer."

"We called it anemia, Dotsie, because I couldn't stand to have you know, but it's real name is leukemia. Which is a form of cancer."

"You can die from it," she said, very matter-of-factly. I started to cry, holding her tightly, but still looking at her. She looked down, thinking, and then she said, incredibly, "I don't know what you're so worried about. I'm going to heaven." Miss Anderson was right. She knew, and she accepted it on some level, and was doing far better at that than I was. And now here she was comforting me.

"Of course you're going to heaven. Me too. And there's a chance you might get well, too. Sometimes it happens. It can always happen."

"But most of the kids in here die, don't they." Her eyes suddenly filled with tears. "I'll get to see Bapa." My father. She let her tears go then, and we both cried together, holding tight to each other, her fuzzy head nestled against my shoulder, our pain somehow easing from having been shared.

When I left the hospital that afternoon, I felt clearer. I wished I had leveled with Dotsie sooner. As sick as my secrets again, I thought, thinking that any hidden agenda, no matter how nobly intended, was wrong. If the road to hell was paved with good intentions, I'd done my best but could recommend that others in the same situation be more honest. At the time, it had seemed unconscionable to tell Dotsie she had a terminal disease. With the accuracy born of hindsight, I could realize I'd been wrong: our communication had suffered, our mutual support had been weakened, and she'd found out anyway.

A week later, as I walked to the elevator after visiting Dotsie, I saw my favorite doctor on the pediatric service. He was one of the warm ones; somehow he hadn't crawled so far into his defenses that he had lost his ability to empathize. He had once told me that he had nightmares about his son getting leukemia, and I knew he found the pediatric service emotionally wrenching and almost unbearable. If it hadn't been for his hope that the experimental drug therapy would bring them closer to a cure, he couldn't have stood it.

"How's everything going?" he asked, as I fell into step beside him.

"She's really sick," I said. "With the side effects more than the illness. The ulceration 5HP causes is really bothering her. When are you going to stop giving her new drugs?"

"I can't do that, you know that. We have a course of treatment we have to follow, and we can't make changes."

"Come on," I said, walking faster to keep up with him. "How can you be so scientific and cold-blooded about it? Why do you have to push things to the bitter end? What do I have to do, take her home? I guess that's what I should do if I can't face more medicine. That's what you'd say, isn't it? If I can't stand the heat, get out of the kitchen?"

"Well, it seems to me I told you once that you had no business in a research hospital. You have to understand what we're trying to do here. And also that a doctor's job is to keep people alive no matter what it takes. Once we lose sight of that, we're in a gray area that's impossible to deal with from a legal standpoint, if not a moral one."

"I *do* understand that. But what about a good death? Pneumonia used to be called the old man's friend. Why do you prolong everybody's agony? For your precious research? And so you can feel you did all you could for the sake of your medical ego, at the patient's expense? You call that ethics? My daughter hurts from these drugs, don't you understand? Is everybody under orders to extend the lives of these children no matter how much pain you're causing them with your lousy medicine? It seems more like everybody's so terrified of death around here that no one's supposed to die. Isn't there such a thing as merciful release?" He looked at me pleadingly and turned to go but I grabbed his sleeve.

"I'm not letting you off the hook," I said. "We have cooperated. You know my ambivalence about using these kids for research, and Dotsie has done her bit for humanity, okay? A year ago, she was one of the first kids to be blitzed by those four major drugs you gave her all at once, and it almost worked for her, and you learned something. If she'd had that treatment when she was first diagnosed, she'd probably be in a permanent remission today. And thanks to her, and children like her, it's working now for others. Isn't that enough of a contribution? She's been on how many other drugs, I don't know. Ten? How about the one where you made the ten vertical and horizontal scratches in the form of a grid on her arm, and rubbed the medicine in?" He flinched. The doctor was hearing me, finally, and had stopped trying to run. "She is extremely weak and uncomfortable, and the ulcers are making it hard for her to eat."

He looked down and sighed, shoving his hands in his pockets and planting his feet solidly. "Okay. 5HP will be the last drug. But we'll have to finish the course of treatment."

I went home that night to Peter and Georgie feeling battered and alone. I was so grateful that he was there, and that I had Georgie, who at least had a chance. That night I called up Georgie's god-parents in New Jersey and asked them to take care of her for me because Dotsie needed my undivided attention. The next day, we drove to their house two hours away, and as we sat in the kitchen over coffee, I felt stretched to the breaking point. I found myself envying Georgie's defenses. She was as unfazed as I'd expected when we left, quietly blending in as if she'd lived in this normal, noisy household of three children all her life. Peter and I left to go home knowing that if she could sense the atmosphere, she wouldn't feel farmed out because she would be cared for by people who had always loved her.

Dotsie's birthday was within a week, and she enjoyed her party in spite of the fact that she did have to be wheeled down to it in her bed with her IV bottle tagging along. She was too weak to get up, and I wondered if she had stayed alive for her birthday. Peter and I blew up balloons until our cheeks were stiff and taped them all over the playroom, and everyone who was well enough came. I played my guitar, singing all Dotsie's favorites and as many requests from the guests as my limited expertise would permit.

* * *

After her birthday, Dotsie was put on the critical list, and I was at the hospital almost all the time. Peter came up after work and we all read and watched television together. It was a quiet time, and it seemed uncanny to me that Dotsie was so at home with Peter, and he with her, that there was no strangeness or tension between them and never had been.

February slipped into March. She had been on the critical list for almost three weeks when I went to see her on March sixth. She was in a private room now, and when I walked in, she looked tired and listless.

"Hi, Dotsie," I said.

"Hi, Mommy." Her voice was soft, almost a whisper. "I feel awful."

"I know, sweetheart. Do you want to come sit in my lap for a while?"

"Okay." She struggled to sit up.

"Don't move, I'll get you." I reached under her and lifted her up in my arms.

"I've got the pole," she said, clanking it along as I walked over to the armchair in the corner and sat down awkwardly, settling her on my lap. The television was on but we didn't really concentrate, we were just cuddling and relaxing together. Suddenly she grasped the right side of her head, and turned to look straight at me.

She said in a clear voice, "Mommy, I've had it." She lost consciousness and slumped against me. Holding her tight, I stood up and walked over to her bed, and with a final tightening of my arms around her, I laid her down gently and covered her up.

I went to the nurses' station to tell them what had happened. When the nurse examined her, she said she was in a coma, and must have had a cerebral hemorrhage, a common occurrence at this stage. She told me to hold Dotsie's hand, that she would be able to sense it. I went over to her bed, sat down, and took her hand in mine, giving the nurse a look that told her I needed to be alone. I looked down at her beautiful, tranquil little face and started whispering the

Lord's Prayer, and when I'd finished, I began it again. I used the Lord's Prayer as a litany and a meditation over the next three days, and it cleared my mind, comforted me, and gave me a handle on the terrible mixture of pain and relief I was feeling. On March ninth Dotsie died, gently and peacefully. "Don't worry, Mommy, I'm going to heaven."

Part Two

Chapter 8

The Ocean

At Dotsie's funeral I was overwhelmed, sitting in the front pew of the huge, somber church, as familiar to me as a school, dark stone punctuated by brilliant stained glass, feeling the press of the crowd behind me. I had expected one tenth as many people.

The three favorite hymns I'd chosen came booming out, and one called "Ye Watchers and Ye Holy Ones" broke me down. When I saw the small white coffin, closed and final, my self-control gave way completely. Peter had to take me out the side door when the service was over. I wanted to get a grip on myself, but when I tried to greet people through my tears, I was barely coherent. I simply couldn't hold up. My faith was obscured by the belief, born of years of agnosticism, that I would never, ever, see my child again. My feeling of missing her was so intense that the knowledge of her permanent absence was absolutely intolerable. I felt cheated, helpless, exhausted, empty, and devoid of any contact with this God I had been so keen on. He simply couldn't exist and allow such suffering and waste, when the wonderful person Dotsie was and was becoming could simply cease to be at the age of eight. And if all the funds used to kill people had been diverted to cancer research

instead, there would have been a cure for her, I was sure. It was a
cruel world, full of evil, and on the day of Dotsie's funeral I wanted
none of it. If it hadn't been for Peter, I would have cracked completely.

Georgie weathered Dotsie's death with considerably more equanimity than I did—in fact, hers was total and alarming. She seemed
not to notice, and looked blank and uncomprehending when I tried
to explain it to her, as if life and death were concepts she couldn't
grasp. She was almost six and had only shown feelings once, when
I had picked her up one Friday at Bellevue a year ago. Her face
had lit up when she'd seen me, and she'd taken off toward me at
a run. I was so thrilled, I had stood there transfixed with my arms
out, thinking, "She loves me." But she had stopped when she was
five feet away, shutting off, and she had never repeated the behavior. So I couldn't tell whether she felt Dotsie's death or not.
Apparently she did not. And yet there was nothing overtly hostile
or deliberately callous about Georgie. With the exception of the
jack-in-the box incident when she was two, she had never hurt
anyone. It didn't seem as if anger or fear were blocking her feelings, in spite of what some of the experts so earnestly proclaimed.
Georgie was simply uninterested in demonstrations of affection,
and yet she must have been happy at home on some level because
she'd only wandered off once, which was par for the course for
toddlers. She knew where home was and she wanted to be there,
if what I picked up subliminally could be trusted. I just couldn't
see her as an "empty fortress" because she was so careful, determined, and constructive. Surely these qualities had their genesis
in her soul, her personal spirit, and her character. They were not
the hallmarks of a hollow child. What drove me crazy was the
mystery of it all, that there were no logical explanations for so
much of what she did and didn't do.

The weeks following Dotsie's funeral were a painful blur.
When Peter suggested I go with him on his next business trip to

Europe, I thought a change of scene and some pampered living would help. Bill was able to assume responsibility for Georgie, overseeing her baby-sitter and making sure she was well taken care of. He had cut down on his drinking to the point where it wasn't noticeable, and had become increasingly supportive, if not financially, at least emotionally. I had long since marshaled my magnanimity, giving up my vendetta, and had prayed for the grace to forgive him. I'd gotten tired of feeding off my bitterness and resentment. And I didn't feel a moral obligation to try to stop Bill in his destructive behavior because he was changing, just as I was. We both wanted a civil relationship, not only for Georgie's sake but for our own.

After I witnessed the impact Dotsie's death had on him, I could no longer blithely label Bill an emotionally frozen sociopath. When he came to the hospital during her last few days, he was always in tears, and I know he must have felt excruciating guilt. I felt sorry for him. I knew that his alcoholism had been largely responsible for his inappropriate and irresponsible behavior, and since the AMA was now calling alcoholism a primary disease genetic in origin, I couldn't very well hold him accountable. It seemed only humane as well as sensible to encourage him to be there for Georgie. And besides, all noble motives aside, I needed him to help me take care of her.

In the summer of 1971, three months after Dotsie died, we joined a beach club on the Atlantic Ocean. Georgie immediately took to spending long periods of time in the shallow end of the pool, hiking along the edge and wafting through the water like a tadpole. But when we would try to take her down to the ocean, she would balk. The waves, which heaved and crashed a good hundred yards away from the pool, seemed to disturb her and she refused to go anywhere near them. "Come on, Georgie. Don't you want to go down to the ocean?" I would ask, cajoling her.

"Georgie not," she would say. When she wasn't in the pool,

she was sifting and digging in the sand near the security of the big wooden fence that separated the pool and the beach.

"Georgie, why don't you want to go down to the ocean? Are you afraid of the water?" She never said the word *yes*, as was typical of autistic children, and she didn't have the ability to explain or describe a feeling or a sensation. I was left to wonder what it could be about the ocean that terrified her, and from such a distance. It couldn't be the sound of the surf, I reasoned, because that was something everyone loved, one of the soothing sounds in nature, more popular than rain on the roof and the wind in the trees. Maybe the sight of the waves overwhelmed her. In Florida, when we were on the Gulf of Mexico in Sarasota, she'd loved going to the beach and playing near the water. And beaches on Long Island Sound hadn't scared her. She had never been exposed to real surf before so it had to be the enormity of the waves. But why did she need to stand back so far? When other children were afraid of the waves, they would at least approach the water's edge, or come within ten feet of it. Georgie seemed to need hundreds of yards. It made no sense.

I walked back to join Peter and Georgie by the pool and saw a friend from Brooklyn Heights. She was someone I'd observed carefully over the last few years because her life seemed to be in the most amazingly perfect order, career and family juggled successfully while living in her magnificently decorated brownstone. And here she was, looking tanned, sleek, and voluptuous in her white bikini as we watched our six-year-olds. I told her about Georgie's unwillingness to go near the ocean. "Oh, I think Georgie will be squared away when *you're* squared away," she said, to my intense discomfort. What did she think, that Georgie had a "roving block of fear" which could attach itself to anything? Or did she think Georgie's unwillingness to approach the ocean was because of a phobia? Did she think that Dotsie's illness and death, and my grief, had caused Georgie's extreme and baffling reactions? Although I knew she was wrong, I didn't know why, and I felt defending my viewpoint was impossible. I sat there with my feet in the water, in a state of desolation.

*   *   *

Peter's children went to camp the first summer we were married, and because we wanted to visit them all and couldn't afford two weeks of motels and meals out, we decided to combine it with a camping trip.

Georgie was a model camper. As curious as a naturalist, she explored the campsite and played endlessly with rocks, twigs, and bugs. She helped me cook in our blackening pot over the fire, and was a good sport about eating our concoctions. One night it poured rain, and Peter had to go out at 2 A.M. and trench the tent to divert the water. Half of Georgie's sleeping bag was wet, but she just curled up at the dry end in a little ball like a caterpillar and slept through it all.

Peter's ten-year-old son, Hunt, was going to camp in Maine, and we thought it would be fun to stop by an aunt's house on a lake nearby. Aunt Ceci greeted us warmly, and insisted we stay for a few days. After Georgie was in bed our first night, we tried to tell her about Georgie's history, but she made light of it, acting as if we'd bought into some kind of psychiatric claptrap. "She's just a normal child who's unusually quiet and shy," she said emphatically, with the authority of age and experience. She refused to believe there was anything wrong with her and we let it go. Georgie didn't do anything overtly inappropriate until the third day when she got into the desk, found my aunt's supply of postage stamps, and stuck them all over some important papers. Aunt Ceci was furious and told Georgie so, but Georgie, who had done it innocently, looked at her blankly and walked away.

"That child ought to be spanked," she said. "Did you see her face when I caught her at it? She just doesn't care! She knows perfectly well what she did. Aren't you going to discipline her?" I felt shot down and helpless, and tried to explain.

"She honestly didn't know she was doing something wrong," I said. "I keep my stamps in my wallet, and don't write many letters, and she's never been interested in things like letters, or any other

kind of communication. The minute she realized she was doing
something wrong, she stopped, and she won't do it again. There's
no need to spank her. Anyway, I never spank her. And she wasn't
being malicious or naughty."

That did it.

"You've *never* spanked her? Why, that's appalling! No wonder
she's so spoiled! Why, she's the most spoiled child I've ever seen!
She knows perfectly well what goes on. She just has you twisted
right around her little finger. Why, I remember when Grafton (her
son, my cousin) pulled that kind of thing on me when he was that
age, and it was a *showdown*. And I *won*. I don't know what would
have happened if I'd given in the way you do." By this time I was
starting to hyperventilate and Peter walked into the room.

"I'm going down to the lake," I said, in as neutral a tone as I
could muster. "You want to come?" We took Georgie and went
down the path where we climbed up onto a rock and looked out
across the water. "Let's go home," I said.

"I heard part of the argument," he said. "She just doesn't understand, and there's no point in trying to explain it. I can imagine
how she feels. Remember, I didn't really get it right away either.
It was so hard to accept that Georgie doesn't communicate properly.
It feels as if she's doing it on purpose, as if she can help it somehow.
And then you gradually realize that she's doing the best she can and
that there's something wrong with her."

"She must think I'm the worst mother."

"Well, you and I know that's not true." He always said things
like that, and it always made me feel better.

We packed up and left within an hour, with me miserable and
wondering if all my relatives felt the way my aunt Ceci did. Did
they even know exactly what Georgie had been like as a baby, or
was like now? Even my closest friends hadn't really known, because
I'd tried either to hide it or to deny it. Evidently I hadn't known
my boundaries as an actress, had written a script to fit the good-
mother image I'd wanted to project, and had compulsively played
the part too well for my own good.

* * *

When we got back to Brooklyn, it was raining, and it kept up for several days. Our usual rainy-day activity was redecorating, and when we decided to tackle Georgie's room, I had a conference with her. "Georgie, you told me that your favorite color was green."

"Green," she confirmed.

Knowing she had trouble with the word *yes*, I said, "Which do you like better, green or blue?"

"Green."

"You like green the absolute best?"

"Green."

"How would you like to go buy some green paint and paint your room green?"

"Paint."

We walked to the hardware store and pored over the color charts. Georgie was fascinated by the little rectangular color samples, touching their smoothness and running her fingers around their edges.

"Georgie, can you find the green?" We had a sheet in front of us which showed thirty shades of green, blue-green, and blue. Georgie pointed immediately to emerald green.

"Which do you like better for your room, this color or this color?" I was testing her, to confirm her choice, and she picked emerald green every time. We bought the paint and supplies and went home.

Georgie, like most autistic children, didn't like change although she never fought me on it directly. So when we moved all the furniture out of her room, she simply got out of the way. My aunt would have been critical because she didn't help, but Georgie had no concept of helping unless it was an activity that interested her. She was not altruistic, and didn't seek approval.

Georgie fixed her attention on the creamy smoothness of the paint, and the thick ripples it made as Peter poured it. She helped us paint, and was careful and dexterous, and between the three of us, the walls were done in an hour. Peter and I painted the woodwork white, and although the emerald green and white gave her room an elegant, bandbox look more suitable for a library than the bedroom of a six-year-old girl, Georgie loved it. When she went to bed that night, she crawled into it as if it were a cave, a peaceful, cozy place of her own.

The next day we wallpapered her bathroom with a benign jungle scene designed for children—cute little monkeys and adorable tigers. When Georgie took her bath that night, she looked like a little wild child at home in her own special universe. It was important to me that—regardless of her deficiencies—I allow her the dignity of her rightful place in that universe, and have faith that she would have her own special contribution to make. As I looked at her in the bathtub that night, I knew I loved her right where she was, allowing her to be who she was, rather than who I thought she should be. It was a good feeling, a feeling of letting go. Who was I, anyway, to be the great dictator here? (Who was anyone, for that matter?) I was only just learning to be comfortable in the world myself, and would have to allow her the space to find her own peace. God had a plan for her life and would choose the road she would travel. I just needed to listen to Him. As I stood there smiling down at her, still wishing she would look at me but understanding that for some reason she couldn't, I said a prayer of relinquishment. Thy will be done, and whatever I'm supposed to do to help, give me the strength to do it.

In July, Evie and Louisa crossed the hall a few times to play, but it was an unsuccessful playtime without Dotsie. And although Georgie and I spent every sunny day at the beach, which might have been a sufficient lure for them, I couldn't bring myself to take anyone out there with us. Socializing of any kind, even with children we knew well, was difficult because Georgie's inappropriate behavior, although often subtle, created an uncomfortable atmosphere. And I bought into it, bringing my own insecurities and fears with me. It was wearing to be with other people for long in a situation like a car ride where I couldn't extricate myself, and the beach was an hour away. Another situation I had trouble with was parties given by people we didn't know very well. Georgie could be counted on to wander around touching people's hair, and to ignore them when they spoke to her. She was also prone to cadging quantities of hors d'oeuvres, her little hand deftly reaching, like a raccoon's paw, around the rim of a passing tray. Some of the guests invariably failed to understand that she was oblivious and disabled, preferring to believe that she was rude and badly behaved. I would imagine them whispering, and once actually heard, "Her mother should do something about her." Yes, please, but what?

Out at the beach, Georgie took swimming lessons from a woman who had been teaching for forty years. Although she was baffled by Georgie, she was so patient and proficient that she managed to teach her how to swim. She said Georgie wasn't able to follow directions, and learned only by trial and error.

One day, when we went to a store for drawing paper, Georgie saw something in an oblong box called "The Body Human." She brought it over to me and stood beside me with it to indicate that this was something she wanted. "Oh, it's a model," I said.

"Model," she said.

"Like a model airplane, only it's a body." We took it home and spread out all the pieces—heart, lungs, kidneys, intestines—on the dining room table. Although it wasn't anatomically correct, the Body Human had a lot to it, and Georgie was fascinated. I worried that some of this interest had been piqued by her trips to Memorial, and hoped it was a healthy obsession. Maybe she'd be a doctor someday.

The Body Human came with brushes and a set of paints in small jars, and together we painted all the body parts. Putting them in place in their transparent shell of plastic skin was like doing a puzzle. Over and over, Georgie would take it apart and put it back together again, snapping in the pieces.

If I hadn't been in and out of denial like a jack-in-the-box, I never would have had the nerve to send Georgie off to first grade in

September. Sure enough, her teacher called me at the end of her second week. "I'd be doing Georgie a disservice if I kept her in my class," she said. "She needs special education." She said Georgie was not teachable in the normal sense, but that she might, in time, be able to learn to read and write if she was specially taught by trained people, one on one or in a very small class. I didn't know where to turn. The League School, the only possibility in Brooklyn, had a two-year waiting list, and when I went carefully through my handbook on special education, there was virtually nothing specifically for autistic children. Finally, I called Bellevue for a referral, and Dr. Campbell urged me to consider bringing Georgie back. "She needs treatment," she said.

Having read and absorbed all of Norman Vincent Peale by now, I tried to practice positive thinking. But it was hard to think positively about Bellevue, even though it was the best place for the treatment of autism in the city—possibly in the world. And if she went elsewhere she would be with children with severe retardation and neurological impairments, and her autism might not be appropriately addressed and treated. Still, Bellevue was depressing and drastic. And how was it going to look on her record, with its negative connotations? Peter understood, but felt that Bellevue meant getting out the biggest guns we could find, and that big guns were in order. With the objectivity and relative neutrality of a stepparent, he refused to minimize the problem, and was only grateful that such excellent help was available. Twenty-two staff to nine kids, I reminded myself. And Dr. Campbell is reputed to be one of the top people in the field. We're not going to find anything as good anywhere else.

I forced myself to make an appointment with Dr. Campbell, and when we arrived, Bellevue was just the same: the fly-specked lobby, ponderous elevators, and chipped blue doors hadn't changed. Miss Dials, poised and splendid, let us in. I made Georgie hold my hand, keeping her on the side nearest the wall, and we ran the gauntlet of the disturbed children's ward together.

Dr. Campbell said she was delighted to see us, and explained that Georgie would be in a class with two other six-year-olds, one of whom we hadn't known before, and who could read. This gave me hope. The doctor marveled at the progress Georgie had made in the year and a half since she'd seen her, and complimented me on how well I had handled her. But she insisted that without treatment and special classes Georgie was virtually ineducable and that Bellevue was best equipped to give her what she needed. Although she felt strongly that Georgie should be an inpatient again, coming home only on weekends, I could only agree to have her come back to the program as a day student.

Georgie seemed as happy at Bellevue as she was anywhere else—except when it came to the blood tests. Routine blood work was part of the regimen at Bellevue. Dr. Campbell found that factors in Georgie's blood chemistry were at the extreme end of every range, and Georgie had a chromosomal abnormality. Georgie, however, did not appreciate these exciting findings and objected vociferously to the invasive procedures that produced them. Although she'd never made repeated and direct verbal objections about anything, she said, "Georgie not like shots," like a litany. Who does, of course, and especially small children. But Georgie's reaction was abnormally intense and protracted, and all the more upsetting because it was mysterious. Dotsie had adjusted to shots and "finger sticks" to the point where she could stick her own finger without flinching. With Dotsie, I had worked out a system involving magic bracelets, magic rings, magic watches, which could take away most of the pain as long as they belonged to someone else (usually me) and could be worn, temporarily, by her. After a while she didn't need them anymore. But nothing seemed to help with Georgie. I wondered if she associated blood tests and the variety of drugs she was given with her sister's illness, and thought she was next. I tried to reassure her although she looked blank when I asked her about it.

Every couple of months Peter went off on a two-week business trip to Europe. Sometimes I went with him, leaving Georgie with Bill, since getting away always did me good and seemed to have no negative effect on Georgie. On one of these trips, we had dinner in Geneva with a couple who were old friends of Peter's. Their youngest child was autistic, and they told us he had just been treated in France for a hearing disorder. They explained that a distortion in their son's hearing had contributed to his autism, and that correcting it had helped. "You should think about it for Georgie. It might help her, too." I tried to be polite but felt they had no idea how serious Georgie's problems were or they wouldn't have suggested something as simplistic as a treatment for her hearing.

"Your son isn't anything like Georgie," I argued. I had seen him several times. "He seems perfectly normal to me. For one thing, he looks at you when he talks. Georgie never does. I'll never forget the way he said, 'Please pass the bread,' and used French, German, and English all in the same sentence. When Georgie was three, she couldn't talk at all."

"But since you last saw him, this doctor diagnosed Henri as autistic," his mother insisted, "and he treated his hearing and Henri is much better. He's more settled down, and relates better with us. He'll be able to learn in school." Those sounded like goals the parents of autistic children have, so I thought I'd at least better ask what this "treatment" involved, even though, in Georgie's case, it would surely be like putting a Band-Aid on a hemorrhage.

"Okay, how does it work?" I asked.

"The doctor does an audiogram and determines where the distortions in the hearing are. He says most autistic children have a distortion and hear certain sounds at a higher volume than we do on certain frequencies, and it upsets them. It hurts them. When he's figured out the frequencies on which the child hears too well, he plays music on that frequency, through earphones, and the child automatically adjusts his hearing so he doesn't hear so well on that particular frequency." It made no sense to me.

"But Georgie's hearing has been tested and it's fine," I insisted. "Anyway, her problems are so severe, I can't see how it would work. She doesn't have anything like the ability to communicate that Henri does. She's much worse than he is, really. You can't imagine."

Realizing they couldn't get through to me, and thinking that perhaps Georgie was too severely autistic to benefit, they turned the conversation to lighter topics. I was relieved. There was no way I was going to whip Georgie out of treatment and off to Europe for some fly-by-night, bizarre, unheard-of treatment—the laetrile of mental health—even if it had helped Henri. By my standards, he was barely autistic. No, I would go the conventional route, without going off on any weird tangents, and I would trust Dr. Campbell. She was the expert, and surely, if this hearing treatment had any merit, she would know about it since treating autism was her sole concern. She was the kind of person who would be up on the latest developments since experimental research was her bag. When I returned from Europe, I didn't even think it worth mentioning to her.

The staff at Bellevue worked tirelessly with Georgie all year, but as June approached, I could see that even with the example of a literate classmate, she was in no way ready to read or write. I could feel bad news coming. On an afternoon in April, when I went to pick her up, a little girl accosted me in the disturbed children's ward on the way to the autistic unit. She was intelligent and appealing, and seemed perfectly normal to me. I wanted to take her home. I asked Dr. Campbell about her and she said she was going to a place called Childville. The word *Childville* struck a nerve. It sounded like the beginning of institutionalization, and that would be the end.

In May, a few weeks before Georgie's seventh birthday, Dr. Campbell asked to see me in her office. When I sat down, she faced me from behind her desk, her hands folded carefully, and her even, perfect features grimly set. Only her eyes betrayed her, showing her concern and her discomfort over what she was about to do. Since Georgie was too old for the Bellevue Program now, but still needed treatment and special education, it was her recommendation and the recommendation of the staff that she go to Childville. She said it was a very good facility, with a high ratio of staff to children, and that only children between the ages of six and twelve were accepted. "No adolescents," she said, as if this were a tremendous drawing card, which I guess it was. I wouldn't have to worry about some big kid making sexual advances. "It has a special education program on the premises although some of the children are able to go to school across the street." When I told her I couldn't handle it, that it would kill me, she said, with a tinge of contempt, "Then you will be keeping her as a *pet*."

Although I sat there with my face in my hands, Dr. Campbell went on to tell me all the good news about Childville: the children were higher functioning than Georgie and could serve as role models for her; she would get constant contact with a peer group; she'd receive therapy twenty-four hours a day. "It will only be for a year or two. You will be happy when you see her progress."

When Peter got home that night, I poured out my anguish. What if Dr. Campbell was wrong, and it didn't work, and I lost her forever to inpatient residential treatment? And how could I bear to part with her? Peter didn't know what to say, torn as he was by what might be best for Georgie and for me, and how I actually felt at that moment. He had picked up my pieces for the two years since Dotsie had died; he knew I was exhausted and burned out, and he wanted me to have a rest. And yet he was afraid that residential treatment was too drastic. Of course Dr. Campbell was the best doctor, and if she was sure Georgie would be home in a year or two, significantly improved, then it would be worth it. As it was, Georgie's future was so bleak we probably should try it. He advised me to take a few days to think it over.

The next day, I was standing in line at the store when someone I barely knew glanced into my tote bag as I was getting my wallet out. It had my usual welter of "stuff" in it—keys, a magazine, a book, Kleenexes, a hairbrush, papers, drawings, receipts, loose change, Bazooka wrappers. "How do you expect Georgie to be able to organize herself when you're in such a mess?" she said.

I stood there frozen, evaluating her remark and looking for the truth that might lie in it: messed-up bag, messed-up kid? It sounded reasonable to me.

I felt dismissed as a mother the day after Georgie's seventh birthday, an overcast day in May of 1972, when she stood by our car to have her picture taken and then drove with me to Childville. When we got there, it looked like an orphanage to me. As we walked up the steps, I felt suddenly overwhelmed by a flash of rage, against whom or what I wasn't sure. All I knew was that to put her in this place infuriated me and made me want to rip lampposts out of the sidewalk. I could barely contain myself as I settled her in her little room on the fourth floor, putting her things away in her bureau, looking out the window at clotheslines and ailanthus trees in the back yards. I hugged her and cried, and wished so hard that she would put her arms around my neck and say, "Don't go, Mommy!" But she had no reaction. It was as if I didn't exist.

Chapter 9

Eagles

*G*eorgie was adjusting, I was told, and she was homesick, so it was best not to see her for a month. Apparently she was spending a lot of time listening to "Nights in White Satin," a song we had often heard while driving and which I hadn't realized she'd enjoyed. And now at Childville she would feel miserable and homesick whenever she heard it, and would cry. Homesick? I couldn't believe it. It felt like a breakthrough to me. I thought, how wonderful, a concrete sign of love (the second one in seven years). But no, that just meant she shouldn't see me, they said, and the sad thing was, there was nothing I felt I could do. I was either going to do this—throw her into a setting where she'd have to find her own way, or keep her home and coddle her, and enable her to be dysfunctional forever. At least that's what Dr. Campbell seemed to think, and I trusted her.

I consoled myself with thoughts of the mother eagle, and how she makes the nest more and more prickly as the eaglets get older, in order to encourage them to fly. And if a little eagle remains in the nest, too scared to move, she ultimately puts him on her back, flies off with him, and dumps him. Then he flies. Hadn't my mother done that with me when she allowed me to be put in the locked ward of a hospital? In some subtle way I'd been clinging to the nest, and she'd had to abandon me in order for me to find my own strength. She hadn't meant it as an exercise in tough love; it had just worked out that way. And now, I felt, I had to do the same for Georgie, even though it felt like swimming against the tide.

Then the doubts would flood in. Was this totally selfabnegating, slavish obedience to doctor's orders really going to work? Would Childville give Georgie the validation of a group, the structure, the attitudes, and the education she needed? Would all this really enable Georgie to make it into the real world? And if having her at home wasn't enough, why wasn't it? When I'd told one friend about sending her to Childville, she'd said, "But we thought you were doing so well with her." That's what I'd thought. But Dr. Campbell said I'd be keeping her as a pet. What had she meant? Was Georgie too shielded and catered to? Did I lack the neutrality and objectivity she needed in order to emerge from her chrysalis? Did I have insufficient faith in her ability to mature? Well, couldn't I change then, and offer her more discipline, more stimulation, more company among children like herself? I was confused, hurt, angry, and aggrieved because my maternal instincts were crying out to protect and nurture her. I felt as if I were being told that what I could give her, which was my best, wasn't good enough.

Georgie did make progress. Her roommates and her "living group" of thirteen girls lured her out of her own world because they needed her as a playmate. They started out with monster (a game of chase), musical chairs, cowboys and Indians, and progressed to lotto and Ping-Pong. Only one of the other children, Emily, was autistic. She had been with Georgie at Bellevue, and I was envious of her mother because Emily was so much more connected and reachable than Georgie, and seemed to have the greater chance.

I began to believe I had done the right thing when Georgie actually began to make friends with some of the other children. Her first friend was a big, bossy girl named Cindy, and she provided a bridge to the other children. Georgie was interacting on an emotional level with her peers, fighting, playing, and "relating for pleasure" for the first time in her life. This was the kind of breakthrough I was looking for, which I felt incapable of engineering, and which I thought was vital if she was ever going to be able to function in a normal community.

One of the children in the living group was a hyperactive, wiry little dynamo with olive skin and dark hair. She was a hellion, always mouthing off at the counselors and swearing like a sailor. Georgie learned some choice words from her, some of them mind-boggling obscenities in multiple syllables, and she learned to enjoy the effect they had on the counselors. Some of the staff were black, and Georgie took to hurling racial slurs at them, enjoying it when they flinched. As a punishment, she would have to stand in the corner for a specific length of time, or sit on a chair facing the wall. Apparently my demure, spaced-out little girl was metamorphosing into an aggressive, foul-mouthed urchin, although she was still ultra-good at home.

Her progress in school was another point in Childville's favor. She went to school on the premises, in a class of four, and her teachers, for the most part, were warm, bright, patient, and capable. When it was discovered that Georgie was severely dyslexic, a remedial reading teacher worked with her for an hour a day. The one-on-one attention Georgie received was rare even in special education, and it eventually bore fruit. Georgie's artwork was also a plus. Her interest, keen eye, and fine hand continued to be evident, partly because of a supportive art teacher who was nondirective and who allowed Georgie full rein in self-expression and choice of media. These were some of the benefits that kept me going, and Georgie made great progress. If the "bliss of growth" was the name of the game, Georgie was succeeding.

Most of the child-care workers who were responsible for the custodial care of the children were kind and loving, and established a bond which the children (and parents) could count on. There were a few, however, who acted like bullies sometimes, and the psychiatrist in charge worried me. He was young, cold, and elegant, and looked like a model from Bloomingdale's Menswear who had mistakenly strayed to the subway. If, as in a school, the headmaster set the tone, there was going to be a clinical, doctrinaire, and misguided side to Childville. He looked as if I could have sat in his office with my hair on fire and his only response would have been to probe my psyche for the covert motives that might have resulted in such interesting behavior. And interestingly enough, his name was Dr. Block. Putting out the fire would never have occurred to him as a solution, as in order for the therapeutic process to achieve its desired result, the patient must learn to put out his or her own fire. This Freudian approach (where everything one ever did, thought, or felt was subject to interpretation in the light of true, subconscious motivation) often had the effect of invalidating feelings, destroying spontaneity, and crippling self-esteem, since no action could ever be taken at face value. Unfortunately, with my "writer's mentality," I knew all about it. It occurred to me that perhaps doctors like this one deserved their own pejorative label, such as refrigerator shrink, or, in keeping with the dignity of the profession, "cryopsychiatrist."

When friends gave us a house out at the beach for August, and Peter's children came to spend the month with us, I was impressed with how nice they were to Georgie when she was there. With their father's remarriage and Georgie's autism on top of Dotsie's illness and death, I didn't know how any of them or us managed to cope. I felt as if I'd been guilty of grandiosity in thinking we could. But Peter always insisted that we were meant to be together, and should just ask God for strength and take each day as it came.

Georgie came home on alternate weekends, and I visited her every other week. When I arrived, if I wasn't taking her home, we would go to a nearby park for an hour or two, and then I would meet with a social worker named Judith, who functioned as our mutual therapist. Judith scared me because she kept insisting that Georgie was schizophrenic. When I insisted that Georgie had been born autistic, she looked skeptical and remained silent, as if she thought I was rationalizing.

Judith seemed to be attached to the idea that Georgie's diffi-

culties stemmed from problems in her environment, and that Georgie had tuned out because of the tension around her. She said that
although the cause of childhood schizophrenia wasn't really known,
environmental and genetic factors in the child's home and the parents' background often seemed to be key. She tried to analyze me,
and I resented it, but went along with it partly out of sheer ignorance,
but also out of fear of not cooperating and having my resistance
devolve on Georgie in some way. The link between autism and
childhood schizophrenia would later be disproven, but at the time,
it was a prevailing theory. Coupled with Bettelheim's theory of
"refrigerator mothers," mom bashing was the game of choice of many
mental health professionals, most of whom had been attracted to
the profession in the first place because of difficulties with their own
mothers. With my egocentricity and self-destructive tendencies, my
attraction toward guilt and blame, and my background as the daughter of the Dear Abby of the teenage world, I was a natural for that
particular bandwagon. It would have taken a miracle to allow it to
pass me by.

Judith was dead set on her theories. Although I knew several
mothers and fathers of schizophrenics who were completely sane,
the incidence of mental illness in the parents of schizophrenic children is high, whereas in the parents of autistic children it is rare.
Obviously, neither Bill nor I was schizophrenic. But Judith, in her
determination to ascribe schizophrenia to Georgie and at least some
kind of craziness to me, was going to ferret out any reasons she
could. I did my best to keep her happy, and became very nearly
awash in the negatives I was able to dredge up from my past,
forgetting about all the good stuff (which was considerable) that had
equipped me and my brothers to survive and contribute. Most dis-
tressing of all, I found myself, after months of arm-twisting, even
agreeing to allow Georgie to be given Stellazine and Thorazine,
major tranquilizers used in the treatment of schizophrenia. It was
frustrating to think they were so locked into their theories on environmental causes. It was hard to believe Georgie was ever going
to get appropriate treatment in this place.

Georgie, in therapy with Judith, was finally able to begin to articulate some feelings. In the claustrophobic, narrow dark-yellow office on the top floor, with its cheap furniture and one grimy window, they would sit opposite each other and try to make some sense of Georgie's problems. Judith remained resolutely aloof and closed, as she had been taught to do.

Georgie told Judith that she thought I had sent her to Childville because she was crazy. "What does that mean?" Judith asked, in her soft-spoken, neutral tone of voice.

"It means violent," Georgie declared. "It's that I have temper tantrums. It's that I yell and swear at the counselors and beat up on kids." She had begun to have tantrums over her homework assignments, among other things, in order to get out of doing them. "My mother put me here because she's mad at me, and because I must be crazy."

"Why is she mad at you?" asked Judith.

"Because I'm crazy?"

"Maybe," said Judith judiciously. No one tuned into the fact that I had crucified myself as a mother for Georgie's sake in order to avoid "keeping her as a pet," as Dr. Campbell had said I would surely be doing if she lived at home. And no one paid the slightest attention to the fact that Georgie was chronically and extremely homesick.

When Georgie had been at Childville for a year, I decided to seek a second opinion while trying to get help for the fact that I'd become a full-blown hypochondriac, coming down with one incurable disease after another to the chagrin and annoyance of my doctor. The psychiatrist I consulted was a Park Avenue type with a huge successful family practice. When we began to work on the guilt that had caused my hypochondria, I asked him to investigate Childville. After conversations with Dr. Block, he told me it was a most suitable place for Georgie, that it was an excellent facility, and that I should be grateful to have her there. Gratifyingly, he said my mental health was fine except for my guilt, and that that would work itself out in time. He dismissed me, saying I was doing amazingly well under the circumstances.

My hypochondria remained intense although I was running out of diseases, so I decided to exercise more strenuously. We rented a house in the Catskills for weekends, and went on long hikes, and in addition to tennis, which I was playing three or four times a week indoors, I took up skating and skiing. Through all this frenetic activity I was always hoping Dr. Campbell's proscribed year or two would turn out to be only one. I was counting the days, hoping that Georgie could come home.

When she was home, though, it was difficult. She was still ultragood—and detached—and I despaired of ever feeling connected to her through affection and conversation. When she returned to Childville after a weekend, I was told she "acted out," and was especially hard to handle on Mondays. "What does she do?" I would ask, and I would hear all about it in such a way as to make me feel in some way responsible.

"Well, she plays 'monster' too roughly, and if she doesn't get her own way, she hits and kicks until people leave her alone. If she thinks the TV's on too loud, she yells and swears, using unbelievable language. In class she can't concentrate and says when it's windy outside that the building's going to fall down. She literally hears things that aren't there. It's good that she's in touch with the hatred and anger she's never dared express at home. She feels safe in doing that here, and this is a good sign." I was also told that she was obsessed with violence and gore and entertained herself with violent fantasies. When she found a doll she would try to destroy it, behavior they found extremely significant and indicative of her hatred of people, engendered by my rejection of her. "But I didn't reject her, she rejected me," I would protest, and Judith would give me a "that's what they all say" look. I was told she was terrified of bleeding to death, and reacted hysterically to the slightest scratch. They felt it was a reaction to Dotsie's illness and death. I agreed with them there, although it was odd and baffling that Georgie had literally never once cut herself or hurt herself at home, even as a toddler, long before Dotsie got leukemia. Judith would often mention Georgie's hyperactivity and dyslexia, but my feeling was virtually to discount them, since they seemed so insignificant in the face of autism, like worrying about hives when somebody has smallpox.

Meanwhile, at home she was too good to be true. Judith would say, "That's schizophrenia." Georgie, with a faint smile on her face, would drift through the rooms of our house in the mountains as ethereally as a mermaid, her hands grazing the furniture. She would putter, and draw, and help me cook, and was amazingly undisruptive, almost as if she were trying to avoid being sent back. She had a long, blue dress she loved to wear, and looked beautiful in it, with her huge blue eyes and wavy hair down to her shoulders. She was compliant to a fault. If I suggested she do a puzzle, she would sit down and set to work. She had been taught how to crochet and do samplers and lanyards at Childville, and would happily work on these things. But she expressed no pride in her work, nor did she offer any reaction to praise. All speech was expressed in a near monotone, without inflection, and her facial expressions were often blank. Sometimes her little Mona Lisa smile would appear and her eyes would light up with fascination over something, a cobweb or a butterfly. But there was never a similar response to another human being or animal. If I said, "What a wonderful cobweb, Georgie. Look at the pattern," the light would fade, and she would shut off. There was no linking up between us, no bridge of commonality, no communion.

We put her on skis, thinking the joy of skiing would do for her what it was doing for the rest of us, and she enjoyed it and caught on amazingly quickly. But Judith said she was "counterphobic," that it was all bravado and really quite dangerous, and would we please keep her off the ski slopes for her own protection (instead of doing what we were doing, which was tantamount to neglect). We treated this piece of Freudian hogwash as gospel, kowtowing to the experts, and confined our skiing from then on to the weekends when Georgie wasn't there.

* * *

Georgie's stay at Childville extended beyond the two-year deadline and her ninth birthday. Judith and Dr. Block were adamant about keeping her there, but I began to look for alternatives. Peter and I investigated suburbs with good special education programs in their public schools, and found in Connecticut what we hoped would be the solution. We moved, fully expecting to enroll Georgie in the local public school, but when her records were received, she was denied admission. "We are not equipped to deal with children like your daughter," I was told. "She is too disruptive. She will be better off staying where she is." I couldn't believe it. Georgie was caught in a revolving door of institutionalization, and I had backed right in, naïvely believing it would only be for a little while.

"They've got us," I told Peter. "Unless we take her out AMA [against medical advice] and tutor her at home. There's no way any school will take her with the kind of recommendations Childville will send out. And even then the truant officer would probably come and send her back."

Not long after receiving this news, I found out I was pregnant. I had wanted a new baby so badly, but hadn't had the nerve until now. I had also wanted to wait until Peter's children were older and Georgie was with us. But now that it was a fait accompli, I was thrilled. With a feeling of celebration combined with a powerful urge to nest (and a warning from the doctor not to overdo it), I quit my job. Since Georgie had gone to Childville, I had worked off and on. The job I had at present, working as an addiction counselor at an outpatient clinic in Brooklyn, was too much of a strain and too long a train ride now that I was pregnant. I gave notice, and when I'd worked my last day and said good-bye to all my patients, I settled down to country living. We had found a house in a romantic setting, surrounded by trees and backing on a winding river deep enough to swim in.

I made curtains and coverlets for the beds in Georgie's room, and when she came for the weekends, we cooked and did puzzles together, but she didn't seem to get much benefit from it. She seemed happiest when she was engaged in her solitary activities, drawing, or playing outside, exploring with her naturalist's eye. She can be a biologist or an entomologist when she grows up, I thought, hoping.

In desperation, Peter and I began going to a church that was known for its healing ministry. We found the services moving and exciting, and they filled a long-felt need. I had always envied certain religious black people and the way they "carried on" in church, with emotion, conviction, and spontaneity. And I loved gospel music. Peter and I were amazed to see emotion in this little church in Darien, Connecticut, which looked so staid from the outside. "The people really get into it," as one friend commented.

Every Sunday during the service I would be moved to tears, and when I'd glance at my husband, he was always crying too, triggered by the exact same thing that had set me off. This was a very special thing to share, crying in all the same places. We would look at each other in absolute amazement.

When the service was over, we would go up to the altar rail where people would pray with us. I was able to suspend my natural reticence, stiff upper lip, and distaste for wearing my religious heart on my sleeve, and allow myself to be nourished and upheld by the prayers. One weekday morning I came to the church and talked with three women for hours in a room by ourselves, telling them my story so they could pray continuously for "healing of memories." They taught me a Bible verse that would stay with me more than any other promise: All things work together for good for those who love God and are called to his purpose. They said that didn't mean things worked out for the *best*, that autism and leukemia could never be thought of as anything but evil, but it did mean that some good could come of them, and that the children (and I) hadn't suffered in vain. It also gave me security and freedom to believe that no matter what happened, or what mistakes I made, God could make everything "work together for good." Like a brass ring on a merry-go-round, I grabbed the verse and held on to it, as a reward (for loving God and being willing to be called to his purpose) and as an incentive (it would keep me going for another ride).

When we brought Georgie to church, she seemed to be fascinated by the way the congregation participated. I could feel her staring at me when I was moved and when I prayed, and when I asked her if she liked it, she said yes. (Georgie had finally learned to say yes, although for years it was "less" for yes, "lellow" for yellow, and "lo-lo" for yo-yo.)

We planned to have her christened, something which we had neglected to do, and were preparing for the occasion when Childville intervened, asking that we cancel the event. They felt it would be too exciting and too confusing for Georgie. One of the ministers at the church was upset by this, and said that it was his conviction, after having prayed about it, that Childville was the wrong place for Georgie. He asked that Georgie be put on the intercessory prayer list, which meant that two hundred people would pray regularly for a sense of direction and for healing. This was a serious group with a documented track record and a high rate of success, and I would be asked to renew my permission every week until a resolution was reached.

Georgie reacted strangely to my pregnancy by gaining weight right along with me. Judith said she was overidentifying with me because she was so infantile, and had never separated herself from me in her head. "But she never was attached to me at all," I said.

"Well, she wanted to be, and must have pretended she was able to be on some level." That I could believe, as I had certainly grown attached to her in spite of the fact that she ignored me completely. Attached or not, I sensed Georgie's jealousy over the baby and could imagine how utterly left out she must have been feeling. And yet she still accepted no affection from me or from anyone else. With her friends at Childville, she never hugged, kissed, or touched. And at home, when the neighbor children ventured to our house or we were invited to friends', it was always the same. "Why's she so weird?" one of them asked me. "How come she won't play?" But Georgie wasn't comfortable enough to play with normal children. She needed her peers around her if she was going to relax enough for that. At home she seemed unable, in any conventional sense, to have a good time. She didn't respond to kidding or jokes, and refused to play even the simplest games. She would persist in her usual activities of drawing, making card houses, and playing outside with anything that came to hand, stones, birds' nests, oddly shaped sticks, shiny pebbles, pinecones, and ferns.

In the summer, when we spanned the river behind our house with a space trolley, a trapeze on a pulley going from one bank to the other between two trees, we thought surely she'd enjoy it the way the rest of us did, rocketing across on the bar and dropping off in the deep water. But she wanted only to play in the shallow water and dig in the sand.

The baby was born on schedule in June of 1975 with no complications, and we named him Mark. He weighed a hefty nine pounds, slept a lot, and was an extrovert from his first cry onward—a normal, healthy, big fat baby boy. I had everything I'd always wanted: natural childbirth with the father present and involved, breastfeeding on the delivery table, rooming in. It was as fulfilling and exhilarating as I could possibly have hoped, and when Mark looked straight at me and smiled the day after he was born, I was euphoric, not only with delight, but with relief. I wallowed in my enjoyment of him, and Peter fell in love with him, too.

When we got home, we put him between us in our bed and let him sleep and nurse there all night until he was ready for a crib and his own room. I was happy that gone were the days of pediatricians warning that you might roll over and suffocate your baby, a theory never borne out by statistics. I had been scared into believing it when Georgie was a baby, and had always nursed her sitting up and wide awake. No wonder I'd gotten so tired. Now the age of enlightened parenthood was upon us. We knew that babies didn't get suffocated by sleeping parents, and "the family bed" was in.

It seemed, after Mark's birth, that I had a special energy which could carry me through anything I felt led to do. I read the New

York *Times* and magazines as usual, but the rest of my reading was confined to Christian books and the Bible (Peter had already read it from start to finish on the commuter train) as I set out like Don Quixote to try to understand "the peace which passes all understanding." I wanted to know more about this. I wanted to research it. And maybe it was so powerful that I wanted to defuse it by blocking my emotions with my intellect.

I took comfort in the fact that Teddy Roosevelt, Lincoln, Washington, and Einstein had also believed in God. The saying "Wise men still seek Him" made me feel less of a Jesus freak and more of a sensible human being who finally had hold of the truth. And when I read the Gospels carefully, I realized that regardless of how men had abused certain passages of the Bible, Jesus had been an out-and-out feminist and integrationist, and couldn't be blamed for slavery or the position of women in the church.

More important than anything else, my belief in answered prayer was broadened and strengthened, especially after the American Medical Association stated unequivocally that studies showed that prayer facilitates recovery (although they didn't know why).

Peter, who had arrived at a similar orientation a few weeks before me, read right along with me, and philosophized and prayed. It didn't seem so strange anymore that we were moved to tears in church and at the movies, during television shows, over passages in books and things people said. I began to understand that "the two shall become one flesh" meant mind as well as body. I hadn't known this kind of spiritual merging and duplicate emotion was possible, and the timing of it was uncanny. If Peter's children were with us, they'd look at us and laugh and say, "There they go again."

When Georgie came up for her first weekend with us after Mark was born, she ignored him. But Judith told us we should never leave them alone in a room together. I trusted Georgie fundamentally and intuitively, but didn't dare trust my own judgment in the face of Judith's warning. So a new barrier arose between Georgie and me as I tried to accept the unacceptable: someone was in my house who might hurt my son.

Georgie played outside in the woods for hours that summer and fall when Mark was a baby. On windy days she seemed particularly involved, tilting her face and gazing at the branches as if she were listening to something we couldn't hear.

Somehow we never worried that she would get lost when she was outside. Even though her IQ had tested at 75 at Childville, she always knew where she was. She hadn't wandered off since the time in Florida when she was almost three, although a few times she did scare me when I had to call her four or five times to come in for lunch or dinner.

Her interest in exploring was unflagging, and she would often bring things to keep in her room. If we asked her, she would point out the striations on a piece of bark, or the symmetry of a fern or a pinecone, as if she appreciated their design in a special way. I thought about how this was typical of people with a naturalistic bent, and must simply be multiplied in Georgie in some way. She seemed just like the stereotype lepidopterists, bird watchers, entomologists: intense, hypersensitive, observant, enchanted, cerebral. Only she was more so.

On the deepest level, I still couldn't label her insane, no matter how much they counseled me at Childville and insisted that accepting it was the only healthy attitude. It seemed to me she was reacting appropriately within the realm of her perception, and simply marching to an extremely different drummer. Otherwise she couldn't have behaved as well as she did, at least at home. I always had the feeling that Georgie was a mystery waiting to be solved.

At Childville, however, they seemed to think it was less of a mystery than I did. Insanity was inappropriate behavior, and much of what Georgie did was inappropriate behavior. Her IQ of 75 didn't help, and her verbal and interpretive skills appeared to be limited, not to mention her ability to verbalize her feelings except through temper tantrums. There was some question as to whether she had any feelings besides rage. In their eyes she was clearly mad, and if left to her own devices as an adult, would no doubt become a bag woman, wandering the streets with her shopping bags, muttering curses and swearing at passersby, with her eyes cast down and her shoulders hunched.

They felt that Georgie's reaction to rain and wind was hallucinatory in that they appeared to be louder to her than they actually were, and therefore the more threatening. She would obsess about her cyclones, hurricanes, and tidal waves until they despaired of her.

Her latest episode of psychotic behavior had underlined their concerns: Not long after Mark was born, Georgie had come up for the weekend and was more sullen than usual. I thought she must have been feeling fierce jealousy. When she got back to Childville, she got furious about something, and wound up throwing herself against the window. "I want to commit suicide," she yelled, and broke down into hysterical sobbing, fighting the counselors fiercely, kicking and screaming when they tried to restrain her. The window was covered with a heavy screen, and Georgie knew this, but nevertheless, it was regarded as an attempt rather than a gesture, and another large black mark went into the record.

Sometimes, though, when I was playing with Mark, cooing at him and looking into his eyes while we lay on the floor, I wished I could just go along with Childville and be done with it, write her off as treatable but hopeless, a "damaged child" destined for institutionalization. I wanted to be able to chalk it all up to bad breaks and get on with my life with Peter and Mark, believing Childville when they said she was a victim of childhood schizophrenia. The pieces certainly fit: violence, acting out, suicidal ideation, detachment, lack of spontaneity, initiative, and affect, introversion, highly detailed and complex line drawings, inability to concentrate, hostility, "inner rage," ambivalence, foul language, stubborn strength, auditory hallucinations, social retardation, developmental lags, low IQ, split personality (well behaved at home, badly behaved at Childville). It did make a very neat puzzle.

But "I smelled a rat," as my father would have said. I was always uneasy, and so was Georgie. There had to be another way.

Chapter 10

Crossroads

Peter's children, who were now all in their teens, came for Christmas and brought equal numbers of presents for Mark and Georgie. They shared in the fun of Mark's first Christmas, watching him as he sat on the floor like a little Buddha, chuckling and making baby noises as he tore up the wrapping paper. He was six months old, and just learning to crawl. Since he was an adventurous type, I was going to have my hands full.

A few months after Christmas, Bob Weeks, the minister at our church who had taken such an interest in Georgie, approached me after the service. "Gail and I want to go down to Childville to see Georgie with you," he said. Gail was one of the more active members of the congregation. I was amazed that they were willing to make this kind of effort, driving for over an hour into New York, but Bob said Gail had prayed and fasted for ten days, and felt "led" to go. I was touched, and glad to have their company, and would be interested to see what they thought of Childville.

At the last minute, Bob was unable to go, so Gail and I drove down together. As we waited in the lobby for Georgie, Gail began to feel uncomfortable. Childville had an oppressive atmosphere. Now she could feel it too. "It can't be right," she said.

We took Georgie out to a secluded area in the park, and when Gail asked her if she could pray for her, Georgie agreed. Gail anointed her forehead with oil from a little vial, and then we both put our hands on her shoulders and prayed. When we were finished, I wondered if I were imagining things when Georgie looked up with a light in her eyes and a look of happiness that I'd never seen before.

The next day Judith called, wanting to know what had happened to Georgie. She said she'd been unusually hyperactive during their session yesterday, and that afterward she had proselytized to anyone who would listen, talking about God and Jesus, and Christ in her heart. "Now you've added religious mania to her many other problems," she said. "Georgie's treatment conference is coming up soon and you and Peter are expected to be there to discuss this issue."

When Georgie came home that weekend, she smiled when Gail spoke to her after church, and although she received her hug in her usual wooden fashion, her face had lost some of its tension. Peter and I both sensed a change.

When we drove down to the treatment conference, thirty staff members were grouped around a long oval table. Many of them were familiar to us, and they greeted us with subdued friendliness. Because they were already seated, and no one rose to greet us, we felt hat in hand, as if we'd been placed at the bottom of a pecking order. But we were ready for them, the Indians against the cowboys. When we were queried about Georgie's new religiosity, Peter sat up as straight as Abraham and said, "We think Georgie's going to get well."

Everyone stared at us in politely contained disbelief, and then looked to Judith for the first comment. She took several beats, cleared her throat, and said patronizingly, "Well, we all certainly hope so, but don't you think you're being somewhat unrealistic?"

"I don't know," Peter said. "I just know it's going to happen, and I believe we'll be proven right in the end."

Sensing an impasse, Judith diverted the conversation to lighter topics like Georgie's schoolwork and her connectedness with her peers.

After the treatment conference we resumed our normal life, expectant as far as Georgie was concerned, but not wanting to force issues or rush anything. Our lives during the week were ordinary and pleasant—Peter commuted to New York while Mark and I swam at the Y, visited with other mothers and babies, and went for long walks. It was a calm and peaceful existence. On the weekends when Georgie came home, we lived quietly, keeping to ourselves for the most part, doing puzzles, drawing, and cooking. Peter's children were in boarding school and college, and we didn't see them as often as before, but when they were with us for a weekend, or for longer periods in the summer, they were supportive of Georgie and affectionate with Mark. Although there were the normal patterns involving tension, jealousy, and abandonment usually present in "blended families," the constant emergency of first Dotsie's and then Georgie's condition mitigated much of this. We were all called upon to be heroic and magnanimous, and Peter's children rose to the challenge with unusual grace and maturity, adding their example of healthy participation in life and a sense of fun which had a positive impact on Georgie.

This wasn't true of normal children who had a choice in the matter. The four children who lived across the street from us, and children we'd met at church and around town, seemed unable to relate to Georgie in any meaningful way.

Georgie had her eleventh birthday, and by the end of the summer, Judith began to prepare us for the course of treatment they had decided on when Georgie would be twelve and too old for Childville. As a countermeasure, I was doing my own fieldwork, and Peter and I were looking at apartments in New York, thinking we could move back to the city and send her to a school we'd heard about which took a few autistic children. We hoped that because it was a private school, we could talk them into giving Georgie a chance regardless of Childville's negative report.

We found an apartment and were on the point of committing ourselves, when the people at Childville said there was no way Georgie could live at home and go to a day school. She was much too low functioning, vulnerable, and dangerous to be able to handle it, they said, and they would be irresponsible and derelict in their duty if they so much as considered it. They insisted that inpatient residential treatment was the only possible choice for her and told me I was living in a dream world. Mark's pediatrician agreed. "You don't want an autistic child living at home when you have a *baby*," he said, scaring me to death.

Judith made arrangements for Georgie to go to Devereux, an attractive facility in Pennsylvania—"the Harvard of residential treatment centers," as she put it—where Georgie would be able to finish her education and live for the rest of her life. We could see her whenever we wanted, of course, and Judith was sure we would be pleased. She felt certain that we would manage to deal with it with maturity and acceptance, knowing that Georgie would have the happiest life possible given her limitations.

I felt hoodwinked, hornswoggled, and betrayed, especially by Dr. Campbell. Here I had fulfilled my part of the bargain and had done everything she had said, and now Georgie was to be relegated to a pretty village for the mentally handicapped where she would weave baskets until she died.

"Why are you so reluctant to even give her a chance?" I asked Judith when she told me how grateful I should be that Devereux had accepted Georgie. "What have you got to lose, your reputation? You act as if you're holding on to her in some strange way, insisting on controlling her destiny." Judith assured me that it was *I* who was holding on to Georgie. "All I'm trying to do is give her a *life*," I said. "And be her mother."

Before I had a chance to gather my forces, a large brokerage house suddenly offered Peter the job of running their office in Geneva. He liked the idea of returning to Europe, and although it was extremely difficult to get a permit to work in Switzerland, his Swiss background would probably make it possible. He wanted to accept the offer, but had to qualify it by informing the company that we had an autistic child in treatment, and that this would make it difficult, if not impossible, to leave the country. They countered by suggesting that we go to Europe to reconnoiter, in hopes that we could find some sort of solution to Georgie's treatment over there. Peter said, "Let's go."

Chapter 11

Signs and Wonders

*E*ven though we couldn't imagine what a trip to Switzerland would yield in the way of treatment, when Peter said we ought to investigate the possibilities, I had to agree with him. Maybe something would turn up on the other side of the ocean. Taking Mark, we flew over and stayed with American friends, expatriates who lived ten minutes from Geneva in a charming old place on the right bank of the lake. From their front garden we could look across acres of vineyards stretching down to the blue expanse of water with the Alps in the distance.

As soon as we arrived, we telephoned Mark's godfather, whose son Henri was autistic, and asked him if he knew of any options we might conceivably have regarding Georgie's education and treatment. Now that we were here, and faced with it, we were not hopeful, but he seemed to take the question in stride and suggested we consult a psychologist, a Dr. Cecile Wuarin. Peter, whose French was better than mine, called her and made an appointment for the following day.

Fifteen minutes after I set out, it poured with sudden rain, and as I'd had to park several blocks away, I arrived at her office with my scarf plastered to my head and water squishing in my shoes. It was in a row of imposing houses with tall French windows in a spare and elegant section of Geneva.

I rode up in an old elevator with iron grillwork, and to my relief, since I wasn't yet sure of myself in the language, Dr. Wuarin (pronounced, impossibly, vwah-ranh) greeted me in English. She took my sopping coat and invited me to sit on the sofa in the living room, which doubled as her office. Persian rugs and faded upholstery gave the room a comfortable atmosphere, an old-world minimalist feeling which I appreciated. No plaques on the wall, no Danish modern furniture, nothing oppressively cheerful and plastic, just dim light streaming from old tablelamps while the rain tapped rhythmically on the windows. She was a Lincolnesque woman in her sixties—tall, serious, and plain—and she sat sedately in the small, antique arm chair on my right.

"Well, now," she said. "It is my understanding that you have a daughter who is autistic. She is in a special school in the United States." I nodded, forcing myself to sit back on the sofa, cross my legs, and relax. Dr. Wuarin's bearing and obvious intelligence made her seem formidable. Then she asked me a strange question, not your usual first question in a session with a psychologist. "Does Georgie have any sensitivity to any noises?"

I hadn't focused on Georgie's sensitivity to sound because it had seemed random. Many loud noises bothered her but just as many did not, and certain soft sounds seemed more troublesome than others. Because there was no pattern, I didn't know what could be wrong. I told Dr. Wuarin about the drain in the side of the Hotel St. George in Brooklyn, and how uncanny it was that Georgie could hear it so clearly and be so disturbed by it, when Dotsie and I couldn't hear it at all from the car.

"This is very significant," Dr. Wuarin said. "That such a noise could upset her to that degree when you and your other daughter could barely hear it, that is very important." Encouraged, I remembered and recounted the time when we'd had to leave our fifth-row orchestra seats during a production of *The Nutcracker* because Georgie couldn't stand the sound of the violins. I'd had to leave seven-year-old Dotsie alone in her seat while I took Georgie to the very back of the theater where she could watch the ballet from the greatest possible distance. "Georgie covered her ears and said, 'That noise, that noise,' loud and clear, whenever the violins would play. *The Nutcracker* does have a lot of violin music."

Dr. Wuarin nodded her head, asked me to go on, and the incidents kept occurring to me. I told her about Georgie's aversion to pipes, and how she was always nervous around them if she could hear water rushing through them. "When we went down to the basement once in someone's house, when she was four, she stopped on the stairs and wouldn't go any further. There was the sound of water rushing through the pipes which criss-crossed the ceiling of the basement playroom. She started to cry and ran back up the stairs. After that, she was always afraid of pipes."

Dr. Wuarin continued to listen with rapt attention as I gave her as many examples as I could, saying how some noises "drive Georgie crazy."

Stopping my flow of words, Dr. Wuarin sat back in her chair and looked at me squarely. "You are quite literally correct," she said. "It does indeed drive her crazy, as you say. Some children, especially autistic children, have an overdeveloped sense of hearing on certain frequencies, if you can think of the hearing as being something like a radio, receiving signals on certain separate stations. It may be that Georgie's stations are abnormal, and that on some of them she hears far too well, as if the volume were turned up extremely high." I mentioned that Georgie was terrified of thunder and rain, and associated them with earthquakes and floods. Dr. Wuarin said this was a typical reaction in children with sound sensitivity, because thunder and rain *sounded* like earthquakes and floods to them. And when I told her about my guitar, and how Georgie would yank it out of my hand and throw it on the floor when she was a toddler, and how she tried to destroy the phonograph by throwing it on the floor, she felt these were especially important because she had been so young at the time. "There were signs of this when she was much younger than that," I said, remembering how she had never wanted to play with rattles or have me wind up the music box in her teddy bear.

"These children," said Dr. Wuarin, "especially the ones who are born with the disorder, find many normal, ordinary sounds uncomfortable and painful. Voices, for instance, often disturb them to the point where they try to avoid the sound of them. Even their mothers' voices."

"Could Georgie have avoided me when she was a baby because she didn't like the sound of my voice?"

"Of course," she said matter-of-factly.

"You mean it wasn't my vibes, or the atmosphere, or how I handled her?"

"Of course not," she said. If this was true, I was going to have a few questions for Dr. Bettelheim, the cryopsychologist of the Western world, but I couldn't think about that now. I was too busy coming up with clues. I began to think about Georgie's fear of the ocean. After she had learned to read, she developed a mystifying fixation about tidal waves, earthquakes, and floods. Was she afraid of the ocean because it sounded like a tidal wave to her? And could it be that rain corresponded to earthquakes and floods? Dr. Wuarin said it was quite possible.

"But when there's so much else wrong with Georgie," I said, "why is this one symptom of abnormal hearing so important?"

"Because it is the key," she said.

"The key to what?"

"The key to her recovery." I sat there stunned. Up until that point, I had been cooperative and interested, but was thinking that Georgie's reaction to sound was only one piece in the puzzle. Dr. Wuarin explained to me that she had personally witnessed the recovery of many children as a result of having their hearing corrected, and that once this "symptom" was relieved, they were able to concentrate, learn, and slough off their remaining inappropriate behaviors because basic communication became enjoyable for the first time in their lives. She said that a doctor in France, the same one who had treated Henri, could train Georgie's hearing so that the ocean didn't sound like a tidal wave anymore.

"How?" I said.

"He is an ear, nose, and throat specialist," she said, "and when he was going deaf himself many years ago, in Indochina when he was a young man, he cured himself of his deafness by playing music on the frequencies where his hearing was inadequate. He found that his hearing adjusted and grew more acute: he was able to pull his hearing up, like learning to hear your baby's cry if you are several rooms away. Also, in the trenches in the war, not everyone went deaf, and that was because their hearing adjusted, and they learned to receive the sounds of the guns less loudly than before, in order to be able to stand it. They adjusted their hearing down, so they heard less well, but only on certain frequencies or else they would have experienced a unilateral hearing loss. The nerves of the inner ear are somewhat flexible either way.

"When the doctor found that his remedy worked so well on himself, he began to treat others, and he also learned that it might be useful in reverse, for people whose hearing was too loud. This has been successful, and a large part of his practice for twenty years has been the treatment of children for 'hyperaudition.' These children are happy when they are diagnosed and discover that not everyone hears the way they do. Since they have always experienced sound in this way, they think it is normal to hear the way they do. And then, when other people are calm in the face of these noises which to them are unpleasant and painful, they think they are abnormal in their way of reacting, and other people say they are acting crazy. Actually they are reacting appropriately according to what they hear. When their hearing is adjusted, the relief that they feel is often extraordinary.

"You must go and talk to the doctor. That is your next step. Then, if you decide to bring your daughter to Switzerland, he will analyze her hearing and determine the exact frequencies on which the distortions occur. He will play music rather loudly at all frequencies except those frequencies which cause her discomfort, and her hearing will adjust to a greater or lesser degree."

Picturing Georgie walking around with earphones on her ears for months, I asked, "How long will it take?"

"Half an hour, twice a day, for ten days," she said. I raised my eyebrows. How could a problem as seemingly vast as Georgie's, which had cost us and her untold hours of agony, possibly be resolved in half an hour, twice a day, for ten days? Dr. Wuarin gave me an example I could understand.

"If you moved next door to a firehouse, and the sirens woke you up in the night, how long would it take your hearing to adjust so that the sirens didn't wake you up anymore?" I said six months. "Yes, but for how many minutes of *actual listening time* would the sirens be sounding in your ears? You would hardly be listening for six months to noise from a siren loud enough to wake you up. You would go mad."

"What you are telling me," I said, "is that the actual listening time would be maybe three minutes a night, maximum. I guess three minutes of sirens for six months would break down to about ten hours, wouldn't it? So half an hour twice a day for ten days is an understandable amount of time, isn't it?" She was following right along, nodding her head. "And anyway, three minutes a night of a siren blasting is probably too high an estimate. A quarter of that, if you confined it to the kind of piercing noise that would actually wake you up."

She wrote the doctor's name and number on a card and gave it to me. "After you see him, we will talk again." We stood, and towering over me despite her flat shoes, she held out her hand. There was a warmth and a spirit of hope in the room, enhanced somehow by the faded harmony of the furnishings, the subdued light, and the rain drumming on the windowpanes. Dr. Wuarin had opened a door, and Georgie and I were going to go through it together.

I walked to the car shaking my head and rejoicing in spite of the inevitable doubts and fears. Could this really be the healing we had believed was coming? Could it really be happening to *us*? Now that it was upon us, even the possibility seemed incredible and irrational. How could all those years of blighted childhood be ending? How could we even contemplate a recovery from something as serious as autism? Was I just deluding myself the way I had with Christian Science? And what about this Dr. Wuarin? Was she making sense or was she just a fanatic with an ax to grind? Did she understand the seriousness of Georgie's problem? And what if this doctor whose name she'd given me was a quack? What was I doing in a strange country, which used a language I had studied but could barely speak, contemplating a move which would be predicated on my daughter's positive response to a medical treatment no American doctor had ever mentioned to me? And what if it didn't work? Dr. Wuarin had said Georgie's hearing would adjust to a greater or lesser degree. What if it were lesser? And assuming we went ahead, what sort of effect would all this have on Mark, who was just over a year old, and who needed a calm, secure homelife with a mother who was emotionally available, not preoccupied with the seemingly impossible task of seeing Georgie through to recovery? How could she possibly metamorphose from a dense, functionally retarded, severely dyslexic, hyperactive, autistic child with a hopeless prognosis into one who behaved appropriately in school and with her family? It was inconceivable, wasn't it?

The doctor's name was Guy Bérard, M.D., whose offices were located in Annecy, a lovely small city in France an hour's drive from Geneva. When Peter and I drove down two days later, talking all the way about the possibilities, we had a sense of pinching ourselves while remaining alert to the pitfalls. A half hour after crossing the border, we broke through the overcast into brilliant sunshine. As we approached the *centre ville*, we could see the glinting turquoise blue of the Lac D'Annecy, ringed by sharp, snow-covered alpine peaks like a jagged coliseum.

Dr. Bérard greeted us warmly with a smile and a firm handshake. A sprightly, cheerful man with a polite and direct manner, there was absolutely nothing of the quack about him. As he explained his methods to us, auditory training began to seem all the more promising. It was particularly reassuring that he was modest about his successes, and stressed that he was unsure as to how much he could help Georgie.

He showed us the soundproof booth, the earphones, and the amplifierlike apparatus for modifying sound and said, "I understand from Dr. Wuarin that Georgie is afraid of the ocean, of the waves, and that she has a particular fixation about tidal waves." I nodded, grateful that I didn't have to go through her history of sound reaction again. "I think the two are connected, and I want you to ask Georgie a question. I want you to ask her if she is afraid of the Atlantic Ocean because it *sounds* like a tidal wave to her. I think she will say yes. And then you should have her hearing tested in New York." I explained that her hearing had already been tested in New York and they hadn't found anything.

"I am certain they did not," he said, "because they did not know what to look for." He suggested that while the test was being administered, we should watch her face to see if she grimaced in pain. "Children with hyperacute hearing usually will not block the sound when they know they are being tested, they usually will not say anything, or scream, or cry, because they know the sound doesn't last long. But they will make faces, you will be able to see pain on her face. Then you will know she needs treatment." I felt a kind of lightness as he said this, a validation many years in coming: there had been something physically wrong with Georgie after all. I began to believe it and take strength from the fact that not only was there a possible remedy, but my intuition had been right all along.

Dr. Bérard explained that, if we brought Georgie to see him, he would do a detailed audiogram which would reveal as accurately as possible the exact frequencies where her distortions occurred. He said she would then sit in the soundproof booth and place the earphones on her head. "I will tell her she must not take them off. I understand that she is old enough and obedient enough to be able to keep them on. It is a problem for small children, especially aphasic ones, who fight the earphones. For them this is often not so effective." When I expressed my doubts about the treatment only taking half an hour, twice a day, for ten days, he dismissed it. "The hearing is capable of adjusting quite quickly. You will see."

We left Annecy and headed back to Geneva, excited and certain that Georgie should have Dr. Bérard's treatment, but apprehensive at the same time. That night over dinner, as we talked it over with our host and hostess, Peter made an unusual statement which was greeted with some derision.

"I have decided to put out a fleece," he said. "I'm going to ask for a sign." He went fearlessly on, even though the sign he was about to request was a most unlikely event, given the fact that Geneva is socked in by cloud cover from October to May, with perhaps two hours of exception.

"If we are meant to come over here with Georgie, I will be able to see Mt. Blanc tomorrow morning." Then he rose, excused himself, and went off to bed, with me trailing behind, muttering to myself. I remembered another prophetic occasion at Childville when he had announced that Georgie was going to get well.

The next day, we all stood with Peter in front of the house at ten in the morning and watched as the clouds lifted from the top of Mt. Blanc.

At six o'clock on our first evening back, I picked up the telephone to make what felt like the most crucial call of my life. Georgie said hello in her usual monotone. She never called me "Mom." It was always just "hello" like a thud, disaffected and cold. But I was always thanking God that at least she talked. What she said was often reasonable and appropriate although always brief and to the point because Georgie didn't talk often for fun. She usually talked to give information. She conveyed facts and feelings only if asked or if something made her acutely uncomfortable. Jokes, nuances, double meanings, hints, hunches, inferences, verbal subtleties of any variety were lost on her. I always had to edit my speech: our communication was like primary colors, simplified, and without shades.

I took a deep breath and asked her the big question. "Are you afraid of the ocean because it sounds like a tidal wave to you?"

"Yes," she said.

I wanted all the churches in the world to ring their bells.

"I don't hear it the same way you do," I said carefully, hoping I could explain it to her. "It doesn't sound like a tidal wave to me. It sounds good. It isn't scary at all. In fact it calms me down. It's a good sound, for me. A beautiful sound. You hear it much louder than I do, so it sounds scary and huge to you. Do you understand?

"You mean the Atlantic Ocean doesn't sound like a tidal wave to you?" How could she be retarded if she could reason this way, I thought.

"That's right," I told her. "You have a physical problem, Georgie. There is something wrong with your hearing. You hear things too loud. And we can have it fixed, there's a way to fix it so you hear the ocean the way I do." Then she delivered an amazingly insightful statement, the first time I'd ever heard her make a deduction.

"I thought everyone heard it that way and coped with it better than me," she said, and there was real feeling in her voice. Her hearing had always been the way it was, so how could she possibly think that anyone else heard any differently than she did?

"You were just reacting to the noise the way you did because it sounded so much louder to you. There's a doctor who can train you to hear normally, to hear the way Mark and I hear, by using music to train your hearing. There's a way of fixing your hearing so that the sounds aren't so loud and uncomfortable for you. You're going to be all right, Georgie." And then she made another unforgettable deduction.

"You mean I'm not crazy?" she said.

I started to cry. Not only did she have enormous insight into her behavior, which I hadn't realized until now, but evidently she had felt inferior because of it.

"No, you're not crazy," I said. It was the most wonderful sentence I'd ever been privileged to say.

Through our family doctor, who thought *we* were definitely crazy to pursue such an oddball, inadequate remedy for something as complicated as autism, we made an appointment with the head of audiology at a hospital reputed to be one of the best in the city. He was frankly skeptical, but agreed to test Georgie and to allow us to observe her.

When we picked her up at Childville, she was still remote and cold when I hugged her, and we could sense her apprehension over the word "test." How could she be expected to grasp the significance of our conversation at the age of eleven, and to believe that, although it hadn't happened yet, she was going to be permitted to do something tantamount to coming up for air?

Georgie's right ear was tested first, and although she didn't cry out, the pain was plainly visible on her face as she grimaced and scrunched up her features. Although I hated to think about what she must have been going through all these years, I wanted to jump up and run around the room triumphantly. Everything Dr. Bérard and Dr. Wuarin had told me seemed to be validated in that one look of pain.

When Georgie's left ear was tested, the reaction was not so intense, although she was clearly uncomfortable when certain sounds were heard. When the test was over, the doctor approached us arrogantly, he positively swaggered, and with a quizzical smile on his face he said, "Beverly Sills would be *thrilled* to hear as well as your daughter. There's nothing wrong with her hearing." Knowing that we were in a situation where no explanation was possible, we thanked him and prepared to leave. "But before you go, we want to test her right ear again. We think she may have pushed the earphones aside for part of it." Georgie, who was sitting at the far end of the room with a besieged look on her face, had heard the doctor's request and gripped the shiny metal arms of her chair when she saw me coming. She looked horrified and refused to co-operate.

"They can't do that," she said. She covered her ears with her hands and leaned as far over to her right as she could, pushing her face against the back of the chair next to her. We told her she wouldn't have to go through it again, and to put on her coat. Then we thanked the doctor and left. We had all the information we needed.

In my next session with Judith at Childville, I wasn't surprised to encounter some resistance to our grand scheme. She was especially evenhanded and soft-spoken, handling me the way policemen talk to suicides poised on the brink. "It's understandable that you might have some difficulty processing your feelings about Georgie's placement in Devereux," she said, with the weight of her two years' experience as a social worker behind her, "even though it's such an excellent facility that I was surprised and relieved when they accepted her. It's very normal to feel some separation anxiety." She leaned forward, clasping her hands on her desk, and looked me in the eye. "But to think that some sort of doctor is going to cure her is unrealistic to the point of being irresponsible. Even if Georgie's hearing is an issue, it's only a small part of her problem. And since it's only one aspect, your treatment plan is inadequate. Not to mention your follow-up."

When I reminded her that Dr. Wuarin, a licensed psychologist with a *Ph.D.* (Judith had a mere MSW) had agreed to do the follow-up, she gave me an uncertain look. "We just want you to realize that if you persist, we feel there will be difficulties from the outset. For instance, Georgie will decompensate on the aircraft."

"She'll what?" I asked, eager for a new tidbit of psychiatric jargon in spite of myself.

"She'll fall apart. She will become uncontrollable. She's afraid of airplanes."

"She's probably just afraid of the way they sound," I said. "And we can help her with that, now that she knows her hearing is different. Anyway, she hasn't ever screamed or run around uncontrollably in my presence in her entire life, so I don't see any reason why she should suddenly start now."

"But often she has manifested unmanageable behavior here. You know she tried to throw herself out the window, screaming that she was going to commit suicide."

"The window was covered with thick mesh, and besides, her reaction was sound-related. She told me that the radios and the television were all blaring, and the noise was deafening for her. She wasn't allowed to turn down the volume on the television, and no one would let her go to her room because she had to 'work on her socialization.' "

The more I tried to explain hyperacute hearing and its ramifications to Judith, the more hopeless it was. She couldn't accept the idea that correcting Georgie's hearing would make much difference, much less give her a chance at a normal life. I suppose it was embarrassing to have to hear about it from me, like an internist being informed by his terminally ill patient of a drug that could cure him. And when I tried to reach her by remarking on how much calmer Georgie had seemed lately, and that this was related to her new understanding of her problem and its possible solutions, she said that Georgie had often had periods where she seemed calmer than usual. "Perhaps you're reading things into her behavior in order to reinforce your own beliefs," she said.

Several weeks later I got word from Georgie's father that the people at Childville were so concerned about our decision that they wanted him to stop us at the airport if we tried to leave the country with Georgie. He said he was having his sister in Paris check up on Dr. Bérard, and when he heard from her, he would let us know. A few days later he called to say that according to his sister, the doctor was reputable. "I'm calling Childville to tell them that I agree with what you're doing," he said, "so I don't see how they can stop you." Another victory.

I was on friendly terms with two local psychiatrists, and called them to enlist their support. They both felt that auditory training made as much sense as anything else, and that we had nothing to lose. They thought there was a good chance it would work because autistic children are often sensitive to sound. When I asked them to help me deal with Georgie when I brought her home, they agreed to be on call. I asked them if I should take her off the major tranquilizers, and one said yes and the other said no, leaving it up to Georgie and me to decide. I didn't see how anyone could say we were irresponsible when we had the approval and guidance of two psychiatrists of their caliber.

Ostensibly to take Georgie for a two-week Christmas vacation, I drove down to Childville one morning in December. Georgie and I packed her suitcase together, and she seemed almost easygoing as she said good-bye to her favorite counselor and waved to the other children on her floor. Emily was there, Emily who had been with Georgie at Bellevue and Childville. She was as quiet and wan as ever, looking toward us with round eyes, never quite connecting. Her wispy hair and bland features hadn't changed much since she was three, and although she'd made progress, she was still profoundly autistic. What chance would she have now, I wondered. In a year's time she would outgrow the Childville program and would be sent elsewhere, and her warm and caring mother, who I'd known for years, would continue to visit faithfully, always loving Emily and never giving up hope.

In the car going home, I asked Georgie if she wanted to stop taking her medicine, and she said, "Yes," emphatically. When I asked her if the drugs made her feel uncomfortable, she was equally emphatic.

"You don't have to take them anymore," I said. She looked at me, as if to consider this new source of authority. I reached over to touch her hand. It was cold. "We're going to live in Switzerland, and you're going to get well," I said, as if to explain why her ship seemed to have a new captain. She didn't react, but continued to look out the window, fascinated as always by the world flashing by.

*   *   *

Christmas of 1976 was the best we'd ever spent, with all the children there, ranging in age from nineteen to a year and a half. Georgie seemed much more comfortable without the drugs, and we all believed together that she was going to make it. My stepchildren were sad to have us leave the country for what might be an extended period of time, but there would be visits back and forth, and they knew we would see them as often as possible. These children, who had cared so much about Georgie, who had included her, nurtured her, and visited her at Childville, were not going to give us any negatives when they could see that this was her chance to get well.

On New Year's Eve we went to our last service at church. Peter, Mark, Georgie, and I rang in the new year together in an atmosphere charged with love and support. The next day we flew to Geneva. On the plane we got four seats together in the middle, and Georgie didn't even begin to "decompensate on the aircraft." She enjoyed the flight, listening to music through the earphones most of the way, leafing through magazines, and even relishing her airline lunch.

Our apartment was in a residential hotel just outside of Geneva, in a quaint cobblestone village. "What, no neon? No sheets of glass? No billboards? No McDonald's?" I asked Peter.

"There's a McDonald's, don't worry. Right near the station." This pleased Georgie. We were in high spirits, and nothing could dampen them, not even the antiquated stove in our kitchen that perched on its long legs like a large cubist bird, or the small, noisy refrigerator with a crusted, open-ended shoebox for a freezing compartment. We knew we were taking risks by coming here. There were no guarantees, Peter's work permit might not come through, his job might not work out, and Georgie's treatment might not be successful. And we were anxious, and tired. But underneath was a bedrock faith on both our parts that we were heading in the right direction, one step at a time down this strange, new road we'd been led to travel.

Chapter 12

Dancing in the Rain

We woke up refreshed, spoke to our accommodating landlady about a baby-sitter for Mark, and left him with the motherly Swiss woman she recommended. We took the road south from Geneva, up into the rolling high country through scrubby farmland where odd rows of townhouses perched on ridges like crows on a fence. We played tapes of religious folk music, singing along in harmony to boost our morale, and arrived in Annecy in less than an hour.

Dr. Bérard's receptionist ushered us into the doctor's office, where Georgie visibly relaxed as he greeted her enthusiastically. He chatted with her as one normal person to another, assuming her potential for recovery and treating her accordingly. She basked in his good opinion of her, and gave him the feeling that she would cooperate completely.

We handed him the results of Georgie's audiogram, and he looked at them carefully. "Oh yes, I can clearly see the hyperaudition," he said. "I will test her myself now but I am sure I will see many distortions." He proceeded, and the resulting graph looked like an alpine mountain range, full of sharp peaks above the normal line and valleys below it. "The treatment will help her dyslexia," he said, pointing out the valleys which indicated hy-*po*-acute hearing, or hearing *deficits* on certain frequencies. "So much of dyslexia in many cases is related to the hearing; it is not only visual. That she says *b* for *v* is an indication, and once she has the treatment, you may see a big change in the way she can read." He pointed to the peaks on the graph. "This is very acute. She hears far too well on these frequencies and this has made her very uncomfortable, in fact it causes her pain. Some everyday noise, which does not bother others, causes her great pain. "But"—he looked at Georgie, who looked back at him—"even though the treatment may be uncomfortable, you must not take off the earphones. Will you promise me that you will leave them on?"

"Yes," said Georgie. He led her to the soundproof booth, instructing her to sit down and place the earphones on her head. He asked us to wait in the waiting room for the half hour the first session would take. He went back into his office and adjusted the dials on his apparatus, carefully adjusting the settings so as to filter out the frequencies to which she was too sensitive. Then he found just the right music that he felt she would enjoy listening to, once the apparatus had removed the painful sounds. The machine somehow manipulated the remaining frequencies so as to exercise and strengthen Georgie's hearing of nonpainful sounds. He would alternate back and forth between the loud and the soft because she wouldn't be able to endure too much of the loud music at one time.

Half an hour later, Georgie emerged, smiling shyly. Dr. Bérard came into the waiting room. "You were very good," he said to Georgie. "You kept your promise. Was it very uncomfortable sometimes?"

"Yes," Georgie said. "It was. The loud parts."

"I am sorry, I know it is difficult. Go and have some lunch and we will see you later." At two o'clock we returned for the second half of the day's treatment. We were given insurance forms to fill out and learned that the entire cost of the auditory training would be $500, 80 percent of which was covered as treatment for a physical disability—a drop in the bucket compared to the rest of my children's staggering medical expenses.

On the third day of Georgie's treatment, I stayed home with Mark, and Peter took Georgie to the doctor. After the morning's session they walked down to the lake and then window-shopped until lunchtime. They found a restaurant near the station, the sort of place that offered a *plat du jour* served on heavy white china. Georgie feasted on what Peter thought was a bland meal, enjoying the oily pommes frites and pale slab of veal. After she'd finished, she began to stare at a woman at the next table who had long silky dark brown hair. It was worn in a thick swirling twist at the back of her head and was fastened with a large barrette. The warm browns and blacks of the tortoiseshell clip undulated asymmetrically, side by side, and the profile of the woman with her pale skin, Roman nose, and long, dark lashes stood out in relief against the glare of the front window.

"Stop staring, Georgie," Peter said in a low voice. Georgie continued to stare, and the woman turned and looked at Peter reproachfully, catching Georgie's eye. Georgie looked down at her empty plate and then swung her gaze back to the sight which so captivated her. Although she had stopped touching the hair of strangers, which she'd done relentlessly until she was seven, she still disconcerted people by staring with such intensity.

"Stop it," Peter hissed at her and instantly thought, "How can I be reacting this way?" Georgie looked at him and then back, maddeningly and deliberately, at the woman with the shining hair. Peter grabbed her shoulder and squeezed hard.

"Stop staring, do you hear me?" Georgie winced, staring now at Peter with eyes wide with fright. He had never punished her physically, and neither had I. We had always glossed over her inappropriate behavior, jollying her away from the object of temptation, laughing apologetically with the helpless shrug understood by everyone who has ever dealt with a handicapped child. "Get out, Georgie," he growled. "Take your coat and get out. Wait for me outside. And don't let me catch you looking in the window for one second, or else." At the back of his mind was the thought that she was going to get well, and disruptive, annoying, or rude behavior could no longer be tolerated, encouraged, or enabled. And Peter also felt that now that Georgie was home full-time, he was losing control of his peaceful, cozy family life, a life of jokes, play, and cuddling—none of which Georgie had ever wanted to engage in. She had been the eternal drag and wet blanket, and now here she was, threatening to take over the atmosphere. Peter was going to try very hard not to let her get away with it.

Even after so few days of treatment, Georgie seemed less distracted and better able to take discipline and instruction. Watching the cars whiz by outside, she waited patiently on the sidewalk. She learned her lesson well, and gave up staring.

After five days of treatment, Dr. Bérard did another audiogram of Georgie's hearing. "It's working," he said, and showed us a new graph where we could see that the sharp alpine peaks had become rounded and undulating. Similarly, the valleys weren't so far below the baseline. "We are getting an excellent result. Her behavior will gradually change, you will see, she will become less rigid, and you will be able to direct her more. She will get some life in her voice. Of course you must understand that she is going to feel some anger. She is going to feel that she has been underwater for eleven years and somebody has decided finally to pull her up. That somebody is *you*." He looked at me, raising his eyebrows as if to say *watch out*. "Usually the child feels a lot of rage as she becomes more physically comfortable, and naturally gets confused about why she suffered for so long. Her tendency is to take it out on her mother."

After ten days, the treatment was over and we had high hopes. The last audiogram was nothing more than a wavy line, and Bérard was very positive about it although he cautioned us not to expect too much too soon. "Her hearing is now within the normal range," he said. "Please let us know how it's going, and call Cecile Wuarin right away to make an appointment. She is very good with these children, and"—he looked at me with understanding—"with their parents." We all shook hands. Although Georgie reacted obliquely to the doctor, and her handshake was tentative, she had a relieved and grateful look about her, and a sense of dignity I hadn't seen there before.

At six o'clock that evening, Georgie suddenly came up to us as we sat in the living room. "Can I go outside and play?" she asked. It seemed like a strange question as it was dark and raining heavily. She didn't normally ask to go out and play, she just went.

"Why would you want to go out?" I asked. "It's dark and wet out there." She was all set, standing in the doorway with her coat and boots on.

"The storm doesn't sound like a machine gun anymore," she said. Peter and I looked at each other.

"Go!" we said, and she was out the door and down the stairs, racing through the lobby and out into the courtyard. Peter and I got up, and went out onto our sheltered balcony. There was Georgie, whirling and pirouetting, her arms outstretched and her palms up, the rain splashing down on her upturned face. Peter and I stood there with our arms around each other and tears streaming down our faces as we watched Georgie dancing in the rain.

Astonishing signs of improvement continued to emerge. Several days later, when Georgie spotted a skateboard in a store, she begged me to buy it for her. She took instantly to skateboarding, her sense of balance making it easy for her. I watched her from our balcony as she carried the skateboard over the cobblestoned courtyard to the smooth pavement of the street, hopped on, pushed off, and was gone. I had never trusted her out of my sight before, and it felt *great*.

She traveled down the gentle grade into the town, and saw some girls who were chatting and playing by the old stone church that was the focal point of the village. They were about her age, and one of them, who was tall and blond, had a spiffy black-and-white checkered skateboard. She called out, *"Salut,"* as Georgie glided by. Georgie stopped, resting a few feet away with one foot on her board, and said,

"Hi."

"You are American?" the girl asked in French, and since "American" in French is easy to understand, Georgie said, *"Oui!"* hoping that wouldn't make them think she could speak the language.

"Tu parle français?" asked the other girl. She was closer to Georgie in height and coloring, with short brown hair cut in a shag.

"Non," Georgie said, and laughed. The blond girl pointed to her chest to identify herself and said, "Natalie."

"Hi, Natalie. *Moi* [she indicated herself] Georgie," she said.

"Bonjour, Georgie," Natalie said, with a grin. Natalie's friend, whose name was Katrine, went through the same procedure. They spent the afternoon skateboarding and getting to know each other with sign language, French, and English. When Georgie came home her cheeks were rosy.

"I made friends with two girls," she said. "Katrine and Natalie."

"How wonderful," I said, hugging her, and she seemed a little more relaxed and less wooden as she hugged me back.

I found myself thinking that perhaps Dr. Campbell had had a point about not keeping Georgie at home—that because Georgie had lived with so many children at Childville she had acquired greater socialization skills than I'd realized.

One of the most satisfying breakthroughs was Georgie's new interest in the pleasure of conversation. In addition to learning everything she could about her family background, she wanted to know more about world history, and asked me about Hitler, World War II, and the Holocaust. She had been told about it at Childville and wanted to know more. She seemed fascinated by the fact that someone's ethnic and religious background could cause their death. As she became less self-centered and self-involved, she grew more concerned with ideas and larger issues, and wanted to know the difference between forms of government and political systems.

We had lengthy discussions about sex and reproduction, discussing it clinically, and I found that there wasn't much she didn't know, although the nouns and verbs she used were more colorful than the ones I chose.

She was also interested in meteorology, and what she had learned about it in the past had defused some of her fear of floods, typhoons, and cyclones. Her curiosity was inexhaustible, as was her fascination with earthquakes, volcanos, and geography. It seemed she not only wanted to know the basic facts about countries and terrain, but the actual shapes of countries appealed to her in a special way. Geology was also an interest. She was always collecting rocks.

She told me she was much more comfortable, that she no longer heard street noises three blocks away, or people flushing their toilets at the other end of the building, or the blood rushing in her veins. These were revelations to me. She said she had always imagined becoming tiny and traveling through the rushing rivers moving inside her, and that she wasn't fantasizing about that so much anymore.

Much became clear as she explained the effect certain sounds had had on her, and mysteries were solved at a rapid rate. When we had made soufflés when she was little, it was the *sound* of the electric beater she hadn't been able to stand, although she eventually got used to it. And the noise of the dishes clanking in the sink had disturbed her as well. She hadn't been able to blow out the candles on her birthday cake because the sound of blowing had been so disturbing. "It sounded like monsters," she said, as had the puffing noise of the drain in the wall. People's breathing had upset her, especially when several adults were in a small room. And she hadn't liked to use her umbrella when we walked in the rain because of the rain drumming on the fabric. These explanations came out over the course of time, during many conversations when memories of them would be dredged up and reexamined. I was particularly relieved when it came to light that she'd hit the little boy over the head with the jack-in-the-box simply because of the bink-bink-bink noise of "Pop Goes the Weasel," which he'd insisted on playing repeatedly. And I was intrigued to learn that she'd spent so much time out in the woods since we'd moved to the country because the leaves "clacked" when they rustled, like castanets. "When I was in class at Childville, the wind outside sounded louder than it does now," she said. "On windy days, I couldn't concentrate at all. I was sure we'd all be blown away. That's why I was so afraid of cyclones and tornados and hurricanes. And floods. Every time it rained, I was afraid it would flood."

She said she'd had so much trouble learning to talk because she hadn't liked the sound of voices, and had trouble accurately hearing certain sounds (e.g., *yes* sounded like *less*). Because there was so much peripheral noise in our house she hadn't been able to think straight. I remembered that I'd often had the radio, the phonograph, or the television on, and Dotsie had been a noisy little girl at two and three. In addition, we had neighbors and traffic, and wind blowing in the huge trees in the back gardens. Georgie said that Bellevue was quiet, and when they taught her words, she could hear them, even though one of her biggest problems had been the sound of her circulation. It all seemed so simple, now that it was out in the open.

Soon Georgie had several friends in the neighborhood. They communicated in a mixture of French, English, and sign language, and spent hours together skateboarding, jumping rope, and playing games. I hadn't ever thought she could possibly be a child who went out, found friends, and had a wonderful time. And in a foreign country, in a new language, would have seemed doubly impossible even a month ago. It was dazzling and awe-inspiring, this rescue from a fate which might have destroyed us both. It was mind-boggling, and sometimes I felt I was losing my balance to the point of becoming disoriented.

And Dr. Bérard was right: Georgie was angry. Even though she was a hundred times more comfortable, she was unable to control her rage against me. Somehow she blamed me, somehow it had to have been my fault that her childhood up to now had been so miserable. I understood, because I had been at least that mad at myself for exactly the same misplaced reasons. She became subtly passive aggressive, so much so that we invented a family word to make it easy and fast to call her on her behavior. When she would suddenly—"accidentally"—jab me in the ribs, scratch my arm, or slam the door in my face, there was always room for doubt. But she looked furtive when it happened, and I would say, "That was a *hig*, Georgie." A *hostile, inadvertent gesture*. She would be instantly unmasked. Instead of tolerating her, and accommodating her, as I had always done before, I would often find myself in an adversarial position. I would tell her, not always fondly, that she was a deceitful creature. It was hard to keep my faith and my perspective. I knew I should refuse to let her push my buttons, that I should know it was part of her process for climbing out of the abyss. But I was not her therapist, I was her mother, and sometimes she made me so angry I wanted to smack her.

One day, when I was talking on the telephone with a friend, Georgie came in from playing outside and interrupted me with a question. I put my finger to my lips, but she persisted to the point where I lost my temper and slapped her, thinking she was an eleven-year-old acting like a six-year-old. We were both shocked and upset. Although she never interrupted me on the telephone again, I wished I could have brought her out of what I (erroneously) perceived as a developmental lag with more kindness and finesse.

When Georgie and I were sitting on the sofa one afternoon and she said, "Mom, teach me how to act normal," I could hear my brothers chorusing, "Good luck, Georgie." From then on (putting life's little ironies aside), whenever Georgie did or said anything "off," we worked on finding a way that was more natural. The difference between now and before was that she was interested in becoming normal. She was motivated. Before, all her energy had gone into coping with the basics, and there hadn't been anything left over for subtleties.

With some coaching, she trained herself to look at people when they spoke to her, to have a firm handshake, to stand up straighter, and to answer questions with a smile. Because she had always focused on patterns on the ground when she walked, she had developed poor posture, and had to spend some time walking across the room with a book on her head in an effort to correct it. We also had many manners drills. One afternoon after lunch when Mark was asleep and Katrine wasn't home from school yet, we sat in the living room and I told her what she was supposed to do.

"Georgie, you come into the room, and I'll pretend I have someone named Mrs. Smith sitting next to me on the sofa. You come up to her and say, 'Hello, Mrs. Smith,' when I introduce you." Georgie politely said "excuse me" (that was from another drill), left the room, and lurked in the hallway until I gave her a signal. She made her entrance, and right on cue she marched up to her, holding out her hand and looking her staight in her imaginary eye.

"Hello, Mrs. Smith!" (big smile). When asked how she was she said, "Fine, thanks, Mrs. Smith. How are *you*?" We did this until it was second nature to her. As she gave up her old truculent ways, and realized that she couldn't get away with being rude or underhanded, her old behavior cracked off her like a shell. The child inside was a nice, responsible young person with a real stake in her family and community life.

Friends advised us that enrolling her in the local public school would be too much for her, and I was sure they were right. She would be lost in a new language, and it surely would be all she could possibly handle to go to a normal school where English was spoken. People I'd met through friends, church, and local organizations seemed to agree that the logical place for Georgie was the International School, with a curriculum in both French and English. In the beginning of February, Georgie and I found ourselves there, waiting for our first appointment.

We were tense. A lot was riding on this, and she visibly braced when the admissions person introduced himself and ushered us into his office. He made us feel decidedly unwelcome as he busied himself with the papers on his desk. Although he didn't look like a bully, with his slight build, waxen complexion, and thin brown hair, he said, "I have Georgiana's records from her residential treatment center in New York. I can't imagine what you expect us to provide for your daughter. What would you like us to do? Baby-sit?" This last word was said with such venom that I winced. But then I rallied, reminding myself that according to Eleanor Roosevelt, no one could make me feel inferior without my permission. I had also been told, "There are no victims, only volunteers," so I squared my shoulders and tried to reason with him, educating him as to the benefits of auditory training. I glanced at Georgie as I talked to him, noticing that she had paled and was fast retreating into immobility. How I wished I hadn't exposed her to this officious man who either enjoyed cruelty or thought she was too oblivious to be hurt by his words.

When I had finished, he said, "I have never heard of this doctor. He is virtually unknown to the English-speaking community here." I was beginning to learn that this golden ghetto referred to as the English-speaking community was a country within a country, with no easy breaching of the boundaries. "I have never heard of auditory training either, and certainly not as a treatment for childhood schizophrenia."

"But she was autistic, and all her symptoms are going away," I protested. He glanced at Georgie, as if her rigid posture and pallor were a testimony to my self-delusion.

"You have been irresponsible in bringing this child to Switzerland." Feeling like diseased immigrants being turned away at Ellis Island, we left with our heads down, embarrassed, humiliated, and afraid for the future. I tried to reassure Georgie, explaining that people just didn't understand about auditory training yet, and that it wasn't her fault, she was fine.

When we got home and I saw Mark, he seemed to confirm that everything really was fine as he laughed and yelled, "Hi, Mommy. Out!" the minute I walked in the door. I took him outside to play on the equipment in the courtyard and Georgie went off skateboarding, knowing that at least in her own neighborhood, she was just another kid on the block.

Peter got home that night after a fruitless day of trying to secure his Swiss work permit. Although he was eligible for this much-sought-after piece of paper—which was generally given only to males of Swiss ancestry like my husband, or to those rare individuals whose job could not be performed by a Swiss—evidently there was going to be a delay and Peter was upset. It didn't help when I told him about the grim reception we'd received at the International School.

The alternative left to us was the Calvert School in Baltimore, which would send study plans so that we could educate Georgie at home. I wrote to them that day, and in the meantime, a friend lent me social studies, geography, and French textbooks and Georgie and I embarked on a home study plan of our own. Every morning we did lessons, and we enjoyed them, although we could see that Mark's interference was going to make things difficult. Georgie was an eager student. She was interested in everything, and especially remarkable were the intricate, accurate maps she produced. She was able to grasp contours, boundaries, and waterways at a glance and duplicate them, down to every last bend in the river.

A few weeks later, in March, I heard about a small special school on the other side of Geneva where English was spoken. Run by a bright, soft-spoken Englishwoman who wore peasant outfits—the first militantly atheistic communist I'd ever known—the school consisted of a two-room building with a classroom and a kitchen, and an acre of grass where the children could play. There were only two students, one who was intelligent but limited physically by a neurological disorder, and the other, who was physically normal but severely retarded. The teacher said she would be happy to take Georgie for the rest of the year. This was exactly what Georgie needed, as she would be virtually tutored in almost private lessons by an expert. But the fact that the best we could do for her was this tiny school with such damaged children was disheartening, and I went home with mixed feelings of relief and defeat. Georgie, on the other hand, was happy about the prospect of going there and had no qualms at all about the condition of her classmates. For someone her age, she had an unusual degree of compassion, and was not about to be put off by anyone who was different or defective.

* * *

Georgie and I had been seeing Dr. Wuarin separately and together several times each week since the middle of January. Every time we had a problem, she saw it as a natural part of recovery, making us feel we weren't alone. When I next saw her, I was still very upset about the special school in spite of my resolve to calm down and have faith. I told her about my frustration at being unable to find decent education for Georgie, and of being unable to shake off the accusation made by the admissions person at the International School. *Had* I been precipitous and irresponsible? Was Georgie's sullen, adolescent behavior, or my response to it, going to improve? The uncertainties of Peter's job, our lack of permanent housing, and general "toddler burnout" were contributing. I let her have my entire list of complaints without letup. She seemed to understand when I told her I felt like someone in a mud slide who believed she would survive, but meanwhile had to find the strength to tunnel up through a mass of sludge, hoping I wouldn't suffocate in the process.

She listened in her contained way, and when I had wound down she said, "In one year you will have your daughter." I would never forget those words: the daughter I had never had. "She will continue at her present rate of progress, which is a very good rate, and she will not be a problem for you anymore." I believed her. And I realized then that Georgie wasn't the only one who was acting immature. I tried to excuse myself on the grounds of years of accumulated strain, but it also helped to remind myself that although I'd been required to be a pillar of strength, I'd never felt I really had what it took. I wasn't a strong, solid type who could move through mine fields with steady and philosophical determination like Peter. I was terrible at taking risks. I was the one who always played the favorite when my father took me to the racetrack, and was happy to break even at the end of the day. Dr. Wuarin understood. "You have been required to be heroic," she said, "and it hasn't been easy. But soon you will be leading a completely normal life."

Several mornings later, I fainted when I reached up to a closet shelf for a sweater. I came to on the floor with Georgie hovering over me in a state of intense distress. "Mom, Mom, wake up!" It was wonderful. I loved it. Before this, although her defenses had thinned, Georgie had still seemed pathologically detached with us, although she behaved with cheerful spontaneity with her friends. It was hard to hug her, and hard for her to hug back, and we all felt it—a barrier that made us uncomfortable and awkward whenever we tried to give or receive affection. She was no longer a little girl, which was part of it; she had begun her adolescence. But there was more to it than that. Dr. Wuarin said it was a common occurrence and would work itself out in time. And now here was Georgie, being a true big sister to Mark, who was beside her and terrified, and she was looking down at me with such genuine concern that I realized she was there for me, and not just the other way around. And she was unquestionably there for Mark as well. Her intense jealousy, for which I hadn't blamed her, was beginning to break up now that she felt like a full-fledged member of the family. Within a month she asked if she could baby-sit for him if we went out at night. "Do you want Georgie to baby-sit for you when Daddy and I go out?" I asked Mark. He laughed and clapped and ran to her for a hug in reply. We didn't go out much, and when we did, it wasn't for long, and our neighbors were always home. But we all felt good about Georgie taking on the responsibility, especially Georgie. She realized she was making an important contribution to the family.

When I went to the doctor about my fainting, he said it was caused by low blood pressure, which in turn he attributed to fear of failure. "I've got it," I said. "Is this where 'cold feet' comes from?" He said it was. He recommended walking as a cure, starting with twenty minutes a day and working up to an hour. I became a dedicated walker.

When we had been in Switzerland for almost three months, the work permit hadn't been granted and our visas were expiring. In order to renew them, we would have to leave the country for a few weeks and we thought the best way for a family of four to spend the time would be to go on a ski trip. It was beyond our means, but Peter's company agreed to pay for it.

We chose a small resort above the tree line in the French Alps, and as soon as we set off, we began to enjoy ourselves. It felt like a real family vacation. Our apartment, a tiny duplex tucked into the mountainside, was as compact and cheerful as the inside of a new boat. We made ourselves delightedly at home in ten minutes, and sprawled on daybeds covered in yellow plaid, watching the sunset and looking at our sweeping view of snow and mountains. Later, with Mark in his stroller, we took the elevator up to the lobby on the top floor, where we found shops, restaurants, and a huge game room full of pinball machines. Georgie loved the games and was instantly good at them, her hand-eye coordination a wonder to behold.

The next day we arranged to have Mark cared for in the nursery, and the rest of us signed up for lessons. Peter and I were intermediate skiers, and Georgie, who hadn't skied as much, took a beginner's class. It was the first time she would be taught by someone who didn't know her history, and I was nervous. But at lunchtime, when we all convened, her instructor gave us nothing but compliments. "Your daughter has a phenomenal sense of balance," he said. And he didn't seem to think her ability was the result of a counterphobic reaction either, the way Judith had at Childville. I remembered how well she had skied several years ago, and how quickly she had learned to skateboard. Her unusual ability must have been why she never fell down when she was little. It wasn't because she was supercareful out of fear, as Judith had thought. She'd probably gotten her talent from her father, who had never had a dancing lesson and yet had walked into leading roles in his first season with the Charleston city ballet.

Within three days Georgie was skiing at our level. We all took our two-hour morning lesson together, and afterward skied to a restaurant in an old wooden hut at the end of a long trail. It had no electricity, was insulated by eight-foot snowdrifts, and was accessible only on skis, with nothing around it but snow and blue sky. Huge logs blazed in the fireplace, the only source of heat, and the smell of freshly baked bread wafted in from the kitchen. A waitress brought us hefty earthenware crocks of onion soup sealed with bubbling cheese, which we washed down with carbonated apple juice. As we enjoyed our meal together, it was hard to believe that Georgie was the same person as the closed little girl who had had to be reprimanded for staring a few months ago. She was so much more open, relaxed, and self-assured, as well as pink-cheeked and lovely in her bright outfit.

Later on that afternoon, we skied past the nursery to check on Mark. He was playing happily, and even waved hello to us when the baby-sitter pointed us out.

The next morning I went off on my own and unwittingly took a class that was too advanced for me. I sensed that I was outclassed when I was on the lift and saw the narrow ridge where we were to be deposited. When I wound up dangling from the lift by my parka sleeve, I figured it was just the beginning. If the instructor hadn't yanked me loose, I would have been hanging by my sleeve over a chasm on the far side as the chair traveled around the giant horizontal wheel of the pulley before starting down. As it was, he grabbed me and ripped me free of my sleeve. I landed in a heap and watched it flap down the mountain like a wind sock. When the class prepared to schuss down the vertical drop, I said good-bye and trudged off along the top of the ridge, looking for an easier way home.

When I got back to the apartment, Georgie was there with Peter. She was crying and holding her arm. "Mom," she said through her tears, "when I was in the lift line this huge French guy hit me with his ski pole for cutting in. He told me to go to the end of the line or he'd hit me *again*!" I sympathized. I knew it happened often in Switzerland and France. Disciplining each other's children, even physically, was acceptable here. I couldn't very well go out and have him arrested for child abuse because not only was it not against the law, it was tacitly encouraged. And besides, to be scrupulously honest, part of me was glad it had happened because I needed all the help I could get!

I told her about my advanced class and what a mistake I'd made in taking it, that we all make mistakes in life but it's what we do about them that counts. For my part, I was going to have the humility to stay where I belonged in ski school, and for her part she wasn't going to cut the line. "At least you're basically a much better skier than I am. You can make your living as a ski instructor when you grow up if you want to."

"Am I that good?" she asked.

"Yes," I said. "You watch. At the rate you're going, you'll be doing most of the expert slopes by the end of the vacation." This was true. She amazed us, and herself, with her form, her endurance, and her total lack of fear. She seemed to be able to fight her way down anything without a trace of recklessness. It was lovely to see.

Chapter 13

Roses

After the ski vacation we were ready to tackle whatever lay ahead. Georgie went to school every day and began to catch up fast academically with the combination of her enthusiasm and newfound ability to concentrate. She soaked up knowledge, her memory was infallible, and her teacher raved about her but was leery of her being able to cope in a normal school setting. "She is still so lacking in basic knowledge," she said, "and she has never been in an academic situation with normal peers. We really don't know how she'll respond."

At home it was like boot camp. We practiced tough love, using discipline as a means of engineering a crisis that she alone could control and mitigate by improving her behavior. As her ability to communicate honestly improved, along with her manners and her posture, her self-esteem increased and her mood improved. We were strict, even to the point where she had to write sentences a hundred times in a notebook for infractions. Having become so teachable, she was able to bring herself through her developmental lags and act her true age. But the problem was to convince a school that she could adjust and do the work in the light of her previous record.

Putting solutions on hold was still hard for me, but I was getting better at it. With the advent of spring, it made us all feel better to go bike riding through the farm fields that surrounded our village. Although I should have known better by now, I was still surprised when Georgie learned to ride a bike in five minutes, and felt that I was guilty of holding her back in just the same way as her reluctant educators. From the minute she mastered it she loved it, and rode everywhere exploring, with us, with her friends, and on her own. She was careful and responsible and observed all the traffic signs, and I realized with a growing sense of appreciation how impossible this simple activity would have been before we came to Switzerland. One, she wouldn't have been interested, and two, we couldn't have trusted her to obey the law, concentrate on what she was doing, or learn how to do it in the first place.

The school year was ending soon, and Georgie's teacher suggested we have her IQ tested at the local child-guidance center since in the Childville report it was only 75. We were all sure it must have risen, but Georgie was still extremely nervous when we arrived at the center. It didn't help when the woman who was to administer it was overtly hostile. She said, well within Georgie's hearing, "This is a child with many problems, and I have never heard of this Dr. Bérard you speak of. I'm sure if what he is doing is so effective I would know about him." Here we go again, I thought. But I tried to explain that because Bérard was breaking new ground with his treatment, he had found only limited acceptance of it within the medical profession, and that this would change after his book was published. She was not convinced.

When the test was over, the woman evaluated it and said, "It seems very odd but her IQ appears to have risen from 75 to 97." I caught Georgie's eye and we started grinning at each other as the woman rattled on. "But I don't understand this and it is really not important as this child has many learning problems." Essentially ignoring Georgie, and directing her remarks to me, she frowned, looked down, and shook her head as she spoke, acting as if Georgie were a brick wall instead of a sensitive eleven-year-old. "What you are doing here with her is dangerous, it is not enough . . ."

But we were too happy to put up with her any longer. We grabbed our jackets and left, and the minute we were outside Georgie said, "Wow! I'm not retarded!" We hugged each other and danced around the sidewalk before we got in the car. I wished Dr. Small could have been there to see it.

Georgie and Mark turned twelve and two, and right after their birthdays, Peter's work permit came through. This meant that we could definitely stay in Switzerland, and that I could indulge my passionate interest in real estate and begin to look for a house. Georgie's school program ended and I decided to enroll her in the day camp of the International School. Any fears I had were unfounded as they took her without question because she looked fine, had a report from our doctor that she was in good health, and as far as they knew, was a nice, normal child.

Georgie loved day camp. She liked being with so many other English-speaking kids, she thought the swimming was fun, and she particularly liked the crafts, at which she was extremely accomplished. After two weeks I asked the people who ran the camp how she was adjusting, and when they told me she was doing just fine, I asked if I could have it in writing. One of the counselors scrawled a brief report on a piece of paper, and handed it to me with a quizzical look, especially when I clutched it like the Holy Grail and stammered a grateful, hat-in-hand thank you.

I wasn't about to offer an explanation. She didn't have to know that I was celebrating the fact that a neutral person, someone who knew nothing about Georgie and who had spent every day with her for two weeks, had given her an official okay. And I couldn't very well tell her that the report convinced me all the more that it was Georgie's *records* that were holding her back, not Georgie herself. She hadn't been crazy—only crazed. There was a difference.

The house we rented was a little dream house for us, romantic and adorable, high up on a hillside, with a tiled roof and French doors opening onto terraces with a view of the lake and the mountains. Best of all, it was near the Geneva English School, where my friend Pat's children went, and where we were certain Georgie would be accepted. Not only was the school an easy walk from our house, but it was ideal for her: small, structured, friendly, and disciplined. But in spite of all the gains she'd made, and no matter how I pleaded, they would not take her. She was too much of an anomaly, an unknown quantity. Although she appeared to be stable, hardworking, and accomplished, they didn't want to risk it. I was crushed. I had been so sure she would get in, and couldn't believe the negativity we were having to cope with. Wasn't anyone ever going to give this child a chance?

I had trouble believing that my hunch about location had been wrong, and wondered if Georgie was meant to go to the French convent school behind our property. But when I made inquiries, I was told that she would not be able to cope with the language.

I drowned my sorrows in hyperactivity, and settled us completely in a week, hanging paintings, arranging furniture, and assembling treasures as a bulwark against the strangeness of foreign living and culture shock. Mark loved having his toys, although some of them he'd outgrown in the six months we'd been gone, and it was fun to have our board games, which Georgie now enjoyed playing, especially Sorry and Parchesi.

On the morning when the last dish was unpacked and put away, I took my coffee out on the terrace, where I could bask in the June sun, read the Paris *Tribune*, and enjoy the view. Georgie had unpacked the microscope she'd received for her twelfth birthday, and had spent the morning looking at slides. Just as I'd settled myself, she called me into her room to show me something.

"Look, Mom," she said excitedly. "Look at all the colors in this." She slid off the chair and I sat down to see what all the fuss was about. I told her I couldn't see any colors.

"It looks like a grayish-white fleck of something to me," I said. She looked crestfallen.

"It *is* a fleck," she said. "It's dandruff. Can't you see the colors?"

"No. It just looks like an ordinary old piece of dandruff to me."

"Keep looking. You gotta see them." I did, and slowly some reds, blues, and yellows emerged, and as I continued to look, they became clearer. I looked up at her with a new insight when I realized she'd seen them right away.

"Do you think you could have the same kind of sensitivity in your eyesight as you did in your hearing?" I asked. "Because I did *not* see those colors. It took me five minutes to see those colors. But you saw them right away. Do you suppose colors affect you more than they do other people? Do you realize you may actually *see* better than most people as well as *hear* better? I think all your senses must be affected."

Georgie was willing to listen, but obviously she wasn't thrilled at the prospect of being different yet again. She busied herself with a piece of fern and a pinecone, probably hoping I'd go away and stop bothering her. But I couldn't tear myself away quite yet, feeling as I did that mysteries were being solved at a rapid rate, with answers I'd been seeking for years.

Much later, I was to read Dr. Carl Delacato's book *The Ultimate Stranger*, which suggested that autistic children are hyper- *and* hypo-acute in all their senses. This would explain why Georgie's vision was 20/200 in one eye, and the opposite in the other. In fact, although she had to wear glasses because of her weak eye, there had never been a letter on an eye chart that she hadn't been able to see with the other one. She saw like an eagle. This must have been why she'd been so fascinated by people's hair.

"Georgie," I asked. "When you see hair, do you see every strand clearly? Does each one stand out like spaghetti in a dish?"

"Yes," she said. "Don't you see them that way?"

I shook my head. No wonder her own world was so fascinating. "You must see lines, shapes, and colors that we don't see." Memories flooded back, Georgie on walks, looking overwhelmed in her stroller, Georgie watching sunsets (and squinting), Georgie loving the color green, the most soothing in the spectrum. I thought of her on our rain walks with Dotsie, and how we'd had to haul her away from looking at oil slicks in puddles. She must have delighted in the swirling colors. I remembered when we'd gone to the merry-go-round, realizing Georgie must have been blitzed not only by the loud, tinny music but by what must have been uncomfortably vivid colors, fun for the normal child but overwhelming for her. She must have been wondering why kids thought this was fun. In school she must have had sensory overload to the point where concentrating was impossible. It was a tribute to her determination that she'd ever learned anything at all.

The more I thought about it, the more things fell into place. She probably played endlessly with the grooved spool when she was a baby because she had liked the smell of the wood, the look of the grooves, the blandness of the beige color, and the fact that it made no noise. When we had cooked and made soufflés together, I'm sure she must have loved the look of the roux, the sauce we'd made, with its creamy, aromatic texture. "You liked the smell of certain foods, and hated the smell of others, Georgie, but what about people? And animals? How did they smell?" She looked sheepish.

"I still have trouble with that," she said. "Dogs and cats. And smells like deodorant and after-shave lotion, they smell so strong to me I can't stand it, and perfume drives me nuts. I can't understand why people wear perfume, and I can smell hand lotion from the next room." I remembered how our cat had slept curled up next to Georgie sometimes, and Georgie had taken no interest in her. One cat had probably smelled like twenty.

"If you don't like animals, how come you like seals? And bugs?"

"Because they don't smell. And for some reason, I liked the sound seals made. It didn't bother me the way dogs yapping and cats meowing did."

"You really began to talk when you were three, then," I said. "Sooner than Einstein! You didn't want to imitate *people*, but you could do a perfect imitation of a seal. And you kept barking like a seal because you were trying to tell us something but we couldn't begin to understand. You must have loved how sleek and shiny they were."

"I did," Georgie said, but I could tell she felt uncomfortable being reminded about barking like a seal. Of course I was delighted to make sense of what had been uncomfortably bizarre, inexplicable behavior. Now that I understood, I could give her full marks for gumption, and even credit for "talking" a year earlier than we'd thought.

Delacato also theorized that the autistic child's sense of touch was distorted and symptomatic of the disorder—that it was insufficiently sensitive in certain areas and too sensitive in others. His contention was that autistic children who banged their heads didn't feel the pain, and engaged in this sort of self-stimulating behavior in order simply to feel something, some stimulus, which made them feel alive. According to Delacato, the autistic child was only trying to train himself to feel. This would explain why Georgie had bumped her head against her crib, and although she hadn't done it hard enough to hurt herself, she must have been trying to feel something. And it explained her lack of interest in being touched, if in certain ways her skin was too sensitive. This "hypertactility" made touching uncomfortable. When I asked her, she said touching made her feel "funny," although it was much better now; she'd gotten used to it as she got older. No wonder she didn't think hugs were as wonderful as some of us did. Between the way people sounded, and the way they smelled, and how it felt when they touched her, no wonder she had "avoided contact" with them.

"But why wouldn't you look at people? What was so difficult about their eyes?"

"There are things that move in people's eyes. And the colors bother me, too. It's still hard for me but I guess I've just gotten used to it."

"Am I understanding it right, then, that you can cope with the problems with the way you see, smell, and taste, and how your skin feels, because the sound is under control? That's what gives you a handle on the rest?"

"The sound was the only thing that drove me crazy because I got so scared of all that stuff, tornados and hurricanes, and sound was going on all the time. It was hard to get away from it. With the other things I could look down, or walk away. But I could always hear the blood in my veins and my own breathing. Breathing through my mouth didn't sound as loud as breathing through my nose." Until she was four, she had always breathed with her mouth open, which had given her a retarded look. "I love what I see although I get tired of looking at it. I could rest my eyes by looking down." She had walked relentlessly with her head down until she was four, and was trained out of it somewhat at Bellevue. Now I understood. This was why she'd had such bad posture.

"So before your hearing was fixed, you couldn't concentrate, and were constantly overwhelmed." She nodded.

"That's why I love to read now." Before her auditory training, Georgie had rarely read for pleasure, but since the spring she'd been reading voraciously.

"And of course you can eat a jar of pickles at a clip and a lemon like an orange because somehow your sense of taste is hy-*po*-acute in certain areas, but you eat broccoli and cauliflower and airplane food without butter or salt and think they're great because some aspects of your sense of taste must be hy-*per*-acute and you're able to pull flavors out of things that the rest of us experience as bland."

"I guess," she said tentatively. She liked having the mysteries of her peculiarities solved, but as a budding adolescent, the last thing she needed was to be singled out as strange. She just wanted to be a normal kid and lead a normal life. So what if she saw all the colors of the rainbow in a flake of dandruff.

In the residential hotel, I had become friends with a housewife from Zimbabwe who was living in Geneva for two years. I had seen her often, and I missed her after we moved into our house. When she came to see us, she would come for tea (made properly, with a pot and tea cozy she'd given me along with careful instructions), bringing her children to play with Mark and Georgie. She was an important part of the community life we were building. Along with other couples we'd met and old friends whom we saw regularly, we felt less lonely and more connected than "before Georgie got well," the buzz phrase we used as a marker in our lives. We hadn't realized how isolated we'd been.

The summer went by quickly. Mark was now two and spent his time in the vast kiddie pool at the local beach when he wasn't playing on our swings or driving his little red car. My stepson Hunt, now a tall sixteen-year-old, came to stay for a few weeks, and was amazed at the change in Georgie. He was particularly impressed by the way she jumped off the twenty-four-foot diving board, especially since she'd always avoided high boards in the past. I was impressed too, since I couldn't get halfway up the ladder without changing my mind.

At a cocktail party in August, we met a member of the board of the Nouvelle École Moser. He told us it was a progressive private school with a four-month intensive program for foreigners whereby children could learn the language well enough to be integrated into their normal classes, on grade level, in French. He said he had heard from our host that we had a daughter who had been treated by Guy Bérard in Annecy. He said there were several children at Nouvelle École Moser who had histories similar to hers and who were doing very well. "We would be glad to have her enroll," he said. Peter and I looked at each other like two people on a desert island watching a helicopter land.

The Nouvelle École Moser turned out to be a modern building half an hour from our house. When we arrived for our interview, the director of admissions put us instantly at ease, and took Georgie off for a private talk while I filled out forms. They did not request her previous records, and I didn't offer them. As we toured the school, we were sure it would be the right place for Georgie. They felt the same way. She was enrolled on the spot, to start in September, and to Georgie's intense relief as well as ours, the problem was solved. And there was a bonus: not only was she going to have a chance at an excellent education, but she would become bilingual in the process.

Georgie loved the school. She worked hard at her French, and by the end of September she was commuting on the bus and the trolley on her own. When I called several times to check on her adjustment, I was always told that she was making satisfactory progress. After three weeks I made an appointment for a conference, and as I approached the school, I felt the old fears rising. But when I asked her teacher how she was doing, he gave me a look of friendly reproach.

"I have no problem with your daughter," he said. "Only with you." He went on to tell me she was doing extremely well, that she was bright, well organized, hardworking, and that the other children liked her. She was expected to finish her intensive French on schedule, and would go into the sixth grade in January.

Among the books I had brought with us to Switzerland was *The Handbook of Special Education*, a standard reference for schools offering special education in the United States. I was all too familiar with its contents. When I got home, I found it in the bookcase, and holding it carefully in both hands, I walked over to the wastebasket in the corner of the living room and dropped it in.

The fall and winter went well, and by January Georgie was fluent in French and more comfortable in the language than either Peter or myself. She adjusted to the work in sixth grade with no problem, and had a B-plus average at the first marking period in the spring. The mood at home was completely different from the previous year, and although there were still residual tensions, there was much better communication and a basic feeling of cozy family solidarity.

Although people told me that practical jokes were mean and not worthy of the behavior of a civilized adult, once in a while I couldn't resist playing one.

Since Georgie's French was so good that she could pass for a native, we decided to have her play the part of a disoriented individual who would come to the door on a rainy night and ask for directions. Since Peter was heavily involved on the board of an addiction rehabilitation facility on the other side of town, she would ask him how to get there. And he, we hoped, would try to oblige her. This would take quite a while since it would be almost impossible to direct her through the labyrinthine one-way streets—all with names but no numbers—that wound every which way through the town.

The rain began to fall one afternoon and Georgie and I laid our plans. She put on my raincoat and high boots, and an old scarf we didn't think Peter would recognize, and found a pair of sunglasses that, along with heavy makeup, would complete the disguise.

When Peter got home that night, Georgie went out through the basement, waited five minutes, and came around to the front door. Peter had just sat down in the living room with the newspaper when the doorbell rang. "I'll get it," I trilled. When I called, "Who is it?" Georgie yelled through the door in rapid French,

"I'm lost." Except *"Je suis perdu!"* sounded much more plaintive and dramatic. When I opened the door with a great show of suspicion, she began talking loudly and earnestly, telling me in rapid-fire French where she was trying to go and sputtering with frustration at not being able to figure out where she was. It was a brilliant performance. I asked her to wait just a minute, and went into the living room to discuss it with Peter. The moment of truth had arrived. To Georgie's and my glee, Peter sighed, shook his head, put down his paper, and went to the desk to find a map of the city. Then, with map in hand, he walked resolutely into the hall and beckoned to Georgie to come inside. She hesitated, fighting for control.

"But please," he said solicitously in his mellifluous French, sounding like Charles Boyer. "Do come in. I'm sure I can explain it to you." Georgie tried not to notice that I had collapsed into hysteria in the corner. It wouldn't have been so funny if Peter hadn't been so overwhelmingly conciliatory and avuncular with this poor, wet, panic-stricken young woman.

As he began to show her the way, carefully tracing the route, she began to lose it. Her shoulders began to shake. But Peter merely thought she was crying, and when he put his arm around her to comfort her, it was too much for her. She whipped off the scarf and glasses, stepped back, and yelled, "Hi!"

Stunned and gasping, with his mouth open in shock, he turned to me, the accomplice. "I was completely fooled," he said, his face a gratifying study in awe and disbelief. "I had absolutely no idea." He congratulated Georgie on her acting and her incredibly fluent French, and said he knew we'd be talking about this for years: it was one for the annals of the family history. Georgie looked more pleased than Sarah Bernhardt on opening night, and I hadn't had such a good laugh in ages. It was another milestone.

In the summer of 1978, when we had been in Geneva for almost a year and a half, we tried to face the fact that because the dollar had fallen, and the American brokerage business had taken a turn for the worse, we ought to think about going home before we ran into serious financial problems. We had never been ones for smooth sailing in this area, but now things were getting critical. Georgie, however, needed more time, time to become completely confident and to establish a track record, so we decided to make any sacrifice to stay as long as we possibly could.

Georgie's thirteenth birthday, celebrated with her friends, was a big success, and she loved every minute of it. She sat at the head of the table, her hair long and wavy and her teeth in braces, looking like any happy thirteen-year-old. I brought in a cake and she blew out the candles without the slightest hesitation. As I looked at her sitting there in the dining room, poised and happy as she held court surrounded by friends, it was hard to believe that she'd ever had a problem in her life. Friends of ours meeting her for the first time couldn't believe she had any sort of difficult history at all. If we talked about it, which we did less and less, they let us know indirectly that they thought we were exaggerating. We didn't feel it was worth arguing about. They didn't need to know, and we didn't need to dwell on it. We just wanted to forget the past and run with our miracle, although of course we would make an exception if someone else's need arose, as in the case of William Kyle.

William was a severely autistic little boy whose parents, Roberta and Don, were referred to me by a mutual friend in Brooklyn

Heights. Roberta, a bright, savvy writer who had been devastated by her son's disability and was willing to go to any lengths to help him, thoroughly investigated the possibility of having William treated by Dr. Bérard. Having learned all she could from me, she was referred to Jane Madel, Ph.D., who was the head of audiology at the League for the Hard of Hearing in New York, as the best possible person to give William an audiogram. Dr. Madel had lengthy experience in giving audiograms to nonverbal children, and could even test babies for deafness. A probable severe hearing deficit was indicated, although his gross hearing when tested had appeared to be normal. In actual fact his responses were too erratic and inconsistent for first results to be reliable.

Roberta went to see Dr. Campbell at Bellevue. When she mentioned Georgie, she asked, "Do you think Georgie was really autistic?"

"Oh yes," said Dr. Campbell. "She was definitely autistic."

"Then what do you think? Should I take William over for this treatment?"

"I cannot offer you any professional opinion, Mrs. Kyle. But if you can afford to go, you have nothing to lose."

On a bright, sunny day in the middle of summer, Roberta and Don arrived with William, for a visit, and William was treated by Dr. Bérard. Although it helped him become more aware of his surroundings, and there were many small improvements, William was too low-functioning to be able to experience the kinds of changes which might have led to a full recovery. Because he was aphasic and essentially unable to be cooperative, it was impossible for Dr. Bérard to pinpoint the frequencies where distortions occurred. William responded exactly as the doctor had predicted: he improved, by not significantly. Roberta and Don went home hopeful, and planned to bring him back again for another round, but William was to retain his hopeless prognosis. In spite of the dissimilarities in our experience, Roberta and I became the closest of friends.

Chapter 14

Going Home

Georgie finished the sixth grade with no problems, and we spent a quiet summer, going on excursions and to the beach. We were experiencing an unfolding of our relationship as mother and daughter, and a strange understanding beyond the norm. Going through something extraordinary and terrible together had forged an unusual bond and gave special value to leading a normal life. We had become survivors, and although we suffered from stress and were sensitive and a little paranoid, nevertheless we savored each day and never took anything for granted.

In September Mark went to nursery school, Georgie began seventh grade, and life eased into a routine. In October, Georgie and I took a four-day mother-daughter trip to Venice and Florence, choosing two places neither of us had ever been before. We stayed in a tiny, raffish hotel in Venice, unable to believe the gondolas floating by below our window, and a quiet, elegant *pensione* in Florence overlooking the Arno and several stone bridges.

On our second night in Venice, we had dinner in the Italian equivalent of a bistro. When we ordered the seafood platter, Georgie ate every bite, even though the food on the plate was gray and unappetizing, especially the octopus. When I said, "This octopus tastes like an eraser," she disagreed. And when she couldn't finish it, she wanted to take her leftovers home for later.

"How do you say doggy bag in Italian?" she asked.

The waiter understood her sign language and gave her her leftover octopus to take back for a midnight snack. She looked so happy when he handed it over that I realized she was beginning to enjoy her special abilities and eccentricities.

Not long after we returned, I found out I was pregnant. The whole family was happy and excited, and we talked at length about what it would mean to each of us to have another little person in the house. Thinking the baby would be bilingual and have dual citizenship, it was all the more upsetting when Peter was notified that the office in Geneva would be closing. We didn't want to move Mark, and especially Georgie, in the middle of the school year, but we had no alternative. Georgie wasn't able to come to terms with it for at least three days, and I couldn't blame her. She was afraid to go home.

By December, we were flying to New York to look for an apartment. It felt ridiculous in a way, to opt for living in such an expensive city when our source of income was uncertain. But it seemed like the right thing to do. I wanted to be near my mother (who was almost incapacitated by Parkinson's disease) and New York was where we felt most at home. We found an apartment, and blithely enrolled the children in private schools, believing that our God, who had pulled off the stupendous miracle of Georgie's recovery, would surely continue to provide for us financially.

We spent Christmas in a European ski area where we were familiar with the terrain and where Mark could attend the same all-day ski school he'd gone to the previous spring. Now that he was a seasoned three-year-old, he performed parallel turns in a racing crouch with the best of them. He could ski handily through any of the hoops placed in the snow at all angles, and considered himself the king of the bunny hill. Georgie by now had so far outstripped us that she was crashing down great vertical crags that left even Peter hysterical at the first mogul. She often skied alone, but would turn up at mealtime without fail. We loved watching her graceful approach as she wound down the hill making S marks in the snow.

Because of the expense of the vacation, we had very few presents, but Mark was too young to care, and Georgie said that if she had to make a choice, she'd choose skiing any day. For Peter and me, it was a welcome break from the mad materialism of Christmas, and a lovely way to end our time in Europe. Although I had to go slowly because I was in the fourth month of my pregnancy, my obstetrician insisted that it was safe because my center of gravity hadn't yet changed. He said the exercise and the fresh air would be good for me, and he was right.

We saw our friends for the last time, promising to stay in touch. Dr. Wuarin gave us a little antique child's chair as a remembrance. When we said good-bye, we couldn't begin to thank her for the difference she had made in our lives. One look at Georgie's face sufficed, she said. We called Dr. Bérard and promised to keep him apprised of Georgie's progress so that he could include it in his book.

When the moving man came to look over our belongings, we asked him to be especially careful of the cradle in which three generations of babies in my family had slept, and to pack the china and crystal extra snugly in the barrels since they were going to be traveling such a long way. The container would be packed on the moving van and then hoisted onto a ship and transported to New York, arriving in mid-February, weather permitting. It seemed like an efficient system.

When we landed in New York, the glacial blasts of air were an adjustment, but the sunshine made up for them, and it was fun to show the children our new apartment. The first thing they did was run up the stairs from our floor to the health club and the glass-enclosed pool on the roof. With a playground like that upstairs, a garden in front of the building, and a garage in the basement for our car, we thought it was an ideal way to live in New York. All we needed was money.

Six weeks after we arrived, I was sitting at home waiting for the furniture to arrive when Peter called me. He told me I'd better sit down. When I asked him why, he said that the furniture wasn't coming. "Well, when *is* it coming?" I asked.

"It's *never* coming," he answered. I sat down. "Are you still there?" he asked.

"I'm here," I said in a small voice. "What happened?"

"It sank. There was a bad storm, and they had some containers lashed to the top deck, and the ship began to yaw. They had to let the containers go in order to save the ship."

"How much insurance did you get?" He named the figure and I gasped. No one could say that the Lord hadn't provided. But I couldn't stop thinking about the water-logged portraits, the cradle, the needlepoint pillows I'd designed and painstakingly worked, the little silver frames for the pictures of my babies, Mark's little red car, Georgie's microscope, and worst of all, the photograph albums. Even though the feeling of being unencumbered by possessions had its points, I didn't think I'd ever get over the fact that we had lost absolutely everything we owned. I could just picture all our things at the bottom of the sea with the fish swimming in and out.

As if it weren't enough to be pregnant and running around replacing everything from thumbtacks to sofas, problems were developing at Georgie's school. Although one of our brightest friends was director of development, and the headmaster was a reasonable man, one of the staff members played rotten apple by insisting that Georgie must still be autistic because it was incurable. Since she had a psychotic son in a mental institution, she was of course very knowledgeable on the subject of mental illness, and she couldn't believe that Georgie had recovered from autism through some strange, unknown training for her hearing. She educated as many of the staff as she could accordingly. It was all particularly undermining since the school was known for its warm, supportive atmosphere and progressive learning environment. And was, in fact, just that sort of place for everyone, it seemed, but Georgie.

As winter turned to spring and her story circulated throughout the school which regarded itself as one big happy family, Georgie began to feel like a black sheep. She felt scrutinized, as if she'd been put under a gigantic microscope as Exhibit A. "Some of my teachers don't think I can do much, Mom. I can feel it," she said. I told her I knew it was hard to do well when no one thought you could. When her PSAT scores were shockingly low because she had absorbed so little general knowledge before the age of eleven, her teachers glommed on to the numbers as a symptom instead of being excited about her current academic ability. And when I complained and explained, it did no good. They just didn't get it.

Georgie made friends with "another oddball" as she put it, and we were proud of the way she handled her problems. Deciding to bloom where she was planted, she wanted to finish out the year (seventh grade), and complete the next year, because the school ended with eighth grade. She could graduate, which would establish a track record for her, and then hopefully she'd get the chance she deserved in high school. Meanwhile, we would hang on to the story about the bumblebee, who, according to the laws of physics, is unable to fly because its wingspan isn't large enough to support its body. But he doesn't know that, so he flies anyway.

When we'd been home for a while and were settled, Georgie decided to walk over to Childville to say hello. I wasn't available that day to go with her, but a cousin who was visiting offered to escort her. Although it was the weekend and the school was closed, she was able to find a few people she knew on the floor where she'd lived. When she got home she said, "They couldn't believe I was the same person, Mom. They were flabbergasted." I could imagine. She said she never wanted to go back because all the children she'd known well had gone on to other institutions, and her two favorite counselors had left. Not to mention the memories.

When I called Judith, our former therapist, to share the good news, she was always unavailable and never returned my calls. If I had been aggressive about it, she might have, but I didn't think it was worth it. At the end of the school year the facility closed. I didn't feel capable of reopening the wound and enduring the inevitable attacks in order to investigate the methods with which Georgie had been treated. I just wanted to get on with my life and forget the past.

In the spring, Peter and I organized a meeting of parents interested in auditory training, but only extremely low-functioning autistic children made the trip to Annecy. We all hoped they would progress as Georgie had, and although they improved, they had started out at a far greater level of dysfunction and their parents were ultimately disappointed. The parents of the higher-functioning children who might have made greater gains weren't desperate enough to make the trip. We solved the problem of raising false hopes and making inappropriate referrals when we found Jane Madel, who had tested William Kyle. Dr. Madel had met with Dr. Bérard, and was investigating auditory training. She was used to innovative methods through her pioneering work at the League in the treatment of deafness, and she felt auditory training was a valid method of treatment. She took on the job of screening potential candidates, sending only those whom she felt would improve significantly. Because the League treats twenty thousand patients a year, all filed alphabetically, she would not be acquiring easily accessible hard data as to results. (Dr. Bérard's identical filing system caused the same kind of difficulty.) However, she sent "many children," and "sent them regularly," and "everyone benefitted to some degree although no one achieved Georgie's startling result." I concluded that although auditory training was valid, there had been other factors, some of them miraculous in nature, which contributed to Georgie's recovery.

I knew I needed more information about children who had recovered, and wished I had obtained the names of the autistic students at the Nouvelle École Moser who were now doing so well. I hadn't wanted to inquire at the time because I thought it would be an intrusion. And although Dr. Bérard had many success stories in his files, I hadn't felt I could ask for access to them, thinking the parents of children who had recovered might not want to discuss the painful issues of the past.

After Georgie's visit to Childville, we went down to Bellevue to see Dr. Campbell. She greeted us with some reservation, unable to reconcile the change in Georgie with her former prognosis. When I touted auditory training, she shot me down, saying witheringly, "She is a very interesting experiment of one." I felt like a giant tsetse fly who had just been swatted for pestering the elephant of the AMA. We felt Georgie had benefitted enormously from the Bellevue program, and we were suitably grateful. But still, it was horrifying to think that the net result would have been a lifetime of basket weaving had we stayed in this country, and still more horrifying to think that this paragon of the profession, renowned for her dedication and expertise, wasn't even willing to *investigate* auditory training. It wasn't as if it had been invented and performed by a psychic surgeon in the Philippines.

Georgie and I were silent as we rode home on the bus while I ruminated on Dr. Campbell's reaction, wondering if American obstetricians had reacted similarly to Marjorie Karmel when she'd had natural childbirth with Dr. Lamaze in Paris in the fifties. I thought there must be parallels here in the Bellevue Autistic Unit. The obstetricians probably couldn't stand the thought that their beloved (albeit weak, hysterical creatures with no backbone) patients had been writhing and screaming in agony *unnecessarily*. Was the same issue at hand in Dr. Campbell's refusal to entertain the slightest interest in auditory training? And was she also embarrassed for having written Georgie off, and defensive for having insisted on Childville as the only possible solution? And too proud to admit that there might now be another, previously overlooked method in the treatment of autism? And was she perhaps also guilty of belief addiction? Of being so attached to her beliefs that she couldn't see the possibility of another way? Whatever the theories, the fact remained that she wasn't about to rush off to Annecy to learn more. She seemed to feel that it was awkward that Georgie had recovered at all, although I could sense that she was struggling for the magnanimity to celebrate it.

And was I any better? I was more stubborn than most. I had heard about auditory training five years before Dr. Bérard treated Georgie, and shuddered to think that I wouldn't have considered it if Peter hadn't been offered a job in Switzerland. I hadn't had the means or the courage to go tootling off on expensive, off-beat experiments. If I were honest, Georgie recovered strictly by the grace of God, or if you don't believe in God, then fate or luck.

Our disappointments with the reactions of the medical profession continued to accumulate. I tried to contact Bettina Merrill, the doctor at Sloan-Kettering who had told me she was switching from pediatric oncology to child psychiatry "because what's wrong with Dotsie has an end to it, but Georgie's tragedy goes on and on and on." Dr. Merrill didn't return my call or answer my letter. I couldn't believe that this woman, who was so competent and receptive, and who had endeared herself to us, didn't appear to be interested in even giving us a hearing. I had the feeling she thought I was being presumptuous.

In the course of an evening spent with friends, I spoke at length to a famous and extremely successful neurosurgeon who was involved in implanting pacemakers in the brains of autistic children. I regaled him with Georgie's entire history, certain that he, of all people, would understand. "Auditory training has validity, I'm sure," he said. "But I'm doing my own thing."

Although I didn't understand why these people weren't more enthusiastic, Bérard explained that they tended to be highly resistant to new concepts, just as Max Planck had discovered. Max Planck, a physicist who won the Nobel Prize, said that he had been disappointed to learn that scientists were largely incapable of grasping new ideas. A new idea could only be understood when a new generation came in for whom it was no longer a new idea! Bérard said he had given up trying to convince the skeptics in the medical profession. "I am too busy helping children to bother with them anymore," he said. "No one will listen to me until I find the time to write a book, and even then it may take decades."

"I may have to write one too," I said.

Our new baby was a big, bright little girl who we named Sarah. She was born in June, and we were all fascinated by her and argued over who got to play with her next. Peter was eager to be the first one to hold her after she was born, and she spent her first twenty minutes of life being cuddled and cooed at by her father (it was his turn to have the primary bonding experience). We kept her with us for the first month in "the family bed" because I was unwilling and unable to let her out of my sight for long, and her daddy doted on her too.

Peter got a job selling research, and we were able to spend the summer on Fire Island. Georgie's response was completely different than it had been when she was little because the sound of the surf no longer disturbed her. She couldn't seem to get enough of the ocean—no more tidal waves for her—and swam more often and for longer periods than anyone else. She became an expert bodysurfer, and when she got boiled by a wave, she would come up sputtering and coughing but ready to try again. As a swimmer she had unusual endurance, not feeling the cold as much as most people did. When she entered an ocean swimming race she came in third, beating out many adult entrants who had swum regularly all their lives.

Georgie at fourteen was slim and beautiful, with sparkling turquoise blue eyes and a long braid down to her waist. Her high cheekbones and thin Roman nose gave her a patrician look, and her smile was irresistible. Since her recovery, her pallor had been replaced by an English complexion of rosy cheeks which turned to tan in a week of sun. When my brother David and his wife Carol visited us, they were thrilled at how well she was. They reminisced about a memorable trip they had made with her four years before, when they had driven her from Childville to Connecticut. "She stared at the back of my head the whole time," David said. "It was spooky."

"It was so frustrating," Carol said, "because you just couldn't get through to her. And now look at her. It's a miracle. I can't believe the change." Another mark of Georgie's recovery was the lasting bond she established with Sarah within a month of her birth. Georgie often helped me with her by taking her for long walks in the stroller and rocking her in the rocking chair on the porch. She was at just the right age, and doted on Sarah like a second mother.

Peter started to teach Georgie backgammon in the evenings, expecting the task would require all his patience since her PSAT math score was so low. Instead, Georgie became a crack player in a week, and within two weeks she beat him so badly and so consistently one night that his sportsmanship was called into question.

In the fall, Georgie entered the eighth grade. Because she was due to graduate in June, we visited several private schools, but they refused her admission on the basis of her test scores and her record. They seemed to sneer at us for having the gall to apply. I felt I was being treated like a benign eccentric, a deluded mother who actually believed that Georgie had been born classically autistic, and who actually believed that she had gotten well.

A friend suggested that Georgie apply to the High School of Art and Design, a public vocational art school with a full high school curriculum that accepted students on the basis of their portfolios, health forms, teachers' recommendations, and records. Test scores were not counted. And since Georgie's history had done nothing but jeopardize her, we decided to finesse it: when asked for her records, I was prepared to say, "Oh, yes, those! Well, they sank!"—a sure conversation stopper (I was beginning to thank God for the sinking of the container). It was a sad commentary on the enabling ability of educators that we had to resort to becoming con artists in order to have her accepted by an appropriate school. "Ignorance ain't what you don't know, ignorance is what you know is so that ain't so" was becoming one of my favorite sayings.

With the help of her art teacher, who was encouraging and

supportive, Georgie got together a portfolio for the High School of Art and Design. The teachers' recommendations section of the application took some finagling, but the headmaster and several key people were on our side. Since Georgie was, in fact, doing work which would result in her graduation, and since her behavior while she had been at the school had been "within the normal range," the teachers agreed to forgo making any statements about her early history.

When it came to the health form, I took Georgie down to our pediatrician, who was also our friend. He saw no problem in stating that her health was fine, and that she had a history of a hearing disorder, corrected successfully in 1977.

When the High School of Art and Design interviewed Georgie, and asked me about her history prior to 1977, I said she had gone to public school in New York (which was true—I just didn't say that it was special education). When I was asked to produce her records, "They sank!" effectively steered the conversation to the preemptive topic as I told the interviewer all about what happens when your container is thrown overboard in a terrible storm.

The school said they would notify us in March as to whether Georgie would be accepted. When March came and went with no word, I tried not to get depressed. Georgie could always go to the regular local public high school and she would thrive there, I was sure. But in April, just to be certain, I called the office at Art and Design. "Oh you never got it?" the secretary said. "She was accepted six weeks ago. It must have gotten lost in the mail." When Georgie came home from school that day, she didn't stop smiling for an hour. We danced around the living room with Mark while Sarah, who was ten months old, clapped her hands and yelled her one word from her highchair: "digga, digga, digga."

Georgie finished the eighth grade in good standing and graduated in June, looking lovely in her white dress as she accepted her diploma and the French Prize. We spent the summer in the mountains, and she worked in the community day camp as the assistant to the arts and crafts counselor. The children liked her, she was good with them, and she enjoyed teaching them things which she was so naturally good at like macramé, knitting, crocheting, and working with papier-mâché.

She began Art and Design in the fall, commuting on the bus just as she had in Switzerland. After six weeks I called the principal to ask for a progress report. I gave him Georgie's name and asked, "Do you know her?"

"Do I *know* her," he answered. "I know *exactly* who she is, and if she stays, she'll be *valedictorian*."

Chapter 15

Full Circle

Going underground with Georgie's history of autism was risky, as keeping secrets tends to be, but we felt it was the most intelligent concession to reality we ever made. As a "normal" teenager, Georgie was able to run with her assets without interference, and was on the honor roll by the first marking period. When I asked about her after the first semester, I was told she was a teacher's dream.

Because there was some tension and reserve in her manner, she wasn't the center of a popular group, but formed a few close and solid friendships. This followed a pattern set in the other schools she'd been to since her recovery. One of Georgie's friends came skiing with us almost every weekend, and Georgie had the patience to teach her to ski. She tried to teach me, too, giving me more advanced instruction and getting me to try more difficult slopes. One day I let her talk me into attempting to follow her down a top expert slope called "Claire's Run." Georgie helpfully told me it was named after a girl who had died there. "She bumped her head all the way down and died of brain injuries, Mom," she said. Georgie went first, and I followed, tipping off the ledge and finding myself instantly out of control. The slope was slick icy crust, and within a hundred feet I had fallen and was rocketing down the hill on my back, unable to stop, with my head doing a lethal tattoo on the ice. The hill was empty except for Georgie, who was a hundred yards ahead of me and way over to the left.

I yelled, "Georgie, break my fall!" and when she turned and saw me, she immediately began traversing the side of the mountain in great lunges in order to get to me before I shot past her. She made it just in time.

"You saved my life," I said, panting and rubbing the back of my head as we lay in a tangled heap. Georgie was positioned below me, the edges of her skis dug in parallel to the slope.

"Yes, I think I did," she said proudly.

In spite of the fact that Art and Design was a New York City public school, there were no discipline problems there. It was a specialized high school with admission dependent on attitude as well as talent and grades. If a student misbehaved, he was expelled and sent back to his neighborhood for his education. There was a wide range of students in the school, and Georgie said that everyone got along. Her friends were from a cross-section of religious and ethnic backgrounds. There were very few cliques and no prejudice expressed (or even felt, as far as she knew) by any one group against another.

Two French families lived in our building on the same floor, and there was much visiting back and forth. One of the mothers and I worked out an exchange arrangement for the summer with cousins of hers in Paris. Georgie would spend July with them in Corsica on vacation, and their daughter would visit us for the month of August.

"No problem, Mom," Georgie said as she packed her bag. She wrote us letters about hiking in the Pyrenees, windsurfing (which she learned in ten minutes) off the coast of Corsica, and trying to get used to ladies going topless at the beach. I pinched myself to think that she could travel so easily and that, in fact, as teenagers went, she was proving to be far easier than most in every area. Because of what she'd been through, her appreciation of life was boundless, and she wanted to extract the utmost from every experience available to her. To think that I'd once tried to cover up what Georgie was like, and now it was all I could do not to constantly boast about her.

After three and a half years of living in New York, it was proving to be too expensive, and the sound of the crickets and the idea of sending the children out to play in the backyard had more and more appeal. We found a Connecticut suburb that was "New York with trees" in feeling, with good public schools, and when we found a big, old house on an acre of grass near the beach, in a neighborhood full of children, we couldn't resist it. In June we said good-bye once more to friends, teachers, and doctors, and embarked on a life in the suburbs, just as we had eight years ago before Mark was born.

Within a week we were sure we'd made the right decision. To have church, school, beach, and community consolidated in one place simplified life. Since Mark was just seven, and needed his independence, it was a relief to be able to send him out to play without worrying about him. When Mark's school in New York had sent home a note recommending that he always carry "muggers money" when he went out, as they'd found that the boys who carried it were "less badly hurt" than those who didn't, I'd said to my husband, "Can we go somewhere else to live?" And in spite of the fact that Peter would have to commute, he'd agreed.

Georgie lent new meaning to the phrase "having an ear for languages." In her new high school she signed up for Spanish, German, and French, excelling in all of them as well as the studio art courses that would help her get into art school.

Georgie had all the normal fears teenagers have about getting into college, but hers were compounded by the fact that her test scores, although they were steadily improving, were still extremely low. There was no way we could explain them away because even though we had moved to a sophisticated community with a progressive and highly rated school system, we still didn't feel we could share her history without jeopardizing the gains she'd made. Georgie was going to have to pass herself off as one of those bright, high-functioning kids who was always on the honor roll but who just didn't happen to test well.

Evidently the tactic worked because she was accepted at her first choice, an excellent school with a four-year program leading to a bachelor of fine arts degree. She was thrilled when she not only got in, but was awarded scholarships and grants which would cover most of her tuition. Her father and his sister volunteered to pay for the rest.

After a protracted period during which Bill had given his attention to Cesar Chavez and the migrant workers, antiwar demonstrations, and soaking up the wisdom of a Yogi who hung out with his devotees in Central Park, he had decided to realize his life-long dream by becoming a landscape painter. He lived alone (with two cats) in a tiny one-room house in an art colony a few hours away. He had become a romantic figure of the town, a starving artist who worked as the town maintenance supervisor in order to support his painting. He was responsible for the upkeep of the public, outdoor areas, and when I brought Georgie to visit him, we would find him in his faded blue jeans, his matching work shirt with the top three buttons undone, and his fine, light hair curling on his neck, mowing the cemetery or heaving the contents of litter baskets into the town pickup truck. This left him free in the afternoons to absorb himself in his meticulous, highly detailed work, painting the luminous landscapes which became a source of pride for Georgie as well as himself.

Georgie and Bill looked alike, right down to their English complexions and Roman noses, and they had the same mannerisms and mellow bohemian quality. "It's not fair," I said to Peter. "She looks like his clone. It's as if I'd had nothing to do with it." But their closeness made me glad that I'd restrained myself from ostracizing (or murdering) him while she was growing up. Although their relationship was minimal in intensity, at least it was in place as father and daughter and there was love between them. When she went to see him, he always took time to examine her work, following her growth as an artist with deep interest. He said her dexterity was uncanny and that she had the eye of a painter who had been working for twenty years.

A few years before, Peter had attempted to adopt Georgie at a time when she felt that her father was being so negligent that she had to protest. But Bill had surprised us by writing a letter which laid the matter to rest forever. He said that if Georgie were adopted, he would cease to exist as a father, and that he couldn't bear. Georgie felt claimed by him after that, and was able to tolerate his passivity with greater equanimity.

Georgie's graduation from high school, although especially mean-ingful for us, seemed like an unexceptional event to her teachers and all but a few close friends. It was strange to think that she was now legally independent and equipped to support herself, and would actually go off to college in the fall.

In late August 1984, when she began college, I relinquished her with difficulty. I was surprised in the face of my intense gratitude by how much it hurt when we said good-bye at her dorm, and by how diminished I felt as a mother.

She had some difficulty in the beginning over finding the right roommate, resolved when she became friends with Selena, "her buddy." They roomed together happily for the duration. At home we all missed her, Sarah especially, who felt a terrible wrench and didn't adjust to her absence for months.

I kept in touch with Dr. Bérard, and Peter and I had dinner with him in New York at the home of another mother whose child had benefitted from auditory training. He was delighted to hear about Georgie's successes although he wasn't surprised. He told me he wanted to include Georgie's history in his book. In 1984 the book was published in French, and on the back cover, with a picture of the author, was the following: "Hearing, which permits us to hear sound, is not only one of the five senses. Human behavior is, to a large extent, affected by one's contact with the universe of sound. In this book, Doctor Guy Bérard shows how auditory perception anomalies can engender dysfunction *far beyond the scope of the hearing sense*. After a study of the correlations between abnormal hearing and dysfunctions as diverse as depression, *dyslexia*, or *autism*, the author presents the hearing re-education method that he has been applying over the past twenty years." (Emphasis added.)

It was through Dr. Bérard that Dr. Bernard Rimland of the Autism Research Institute (formerly, the Institute for Child Behavior Research) in San Diego discovered Georgie. *Infantile Autism*, Rimland's definitive text on the nature and etiology of autism, was published in 1966 and was the primary instrument in the debunking of Bettelheim's "pernicious" (Rimland's apt word) theories on the cause of autism. He had founded the National Society for Autistic Children in 1965, and was regarded as the foremost authority on the disorder with over six thousand case histories in his computer files.

I wish I had seen his letter to the editor in the New York *Times* when Bruno Bettelheim's book *The Empty Fortress* was originally published. Dr. Rimland had written a rebuttal to the *Times* review claiming that "Bettelheim's ideas about the causes of infantile autism . . . are based on totally unsupported speculation rather than on any factual evidence. To heap guilt, based on disproven, circumstantial evidence, on these parents is an act of irresponsible cruelty."

In his own book, Rimland says, ". . . there is no need for the parents of these [autistic] children to suffer the shame, guilt, inconvenience, financial expense and marital discord which so often accompany the assumption of psychogenetic etiology."

If only I had heard of Dr. Rimland twenty years before!

Rimland helped clarify the distinction between autism and schizophrenia, describing them as completely separate disorders. According to Rimland, schizophrenia is caused by a chemical imbalance which is innate, whereas early infantile autism is defined as being present "from the beginning of life." As James Roy Morrison, M.D., corroborates in *Brother's Keeper*, his guide for families dealing with the mentally ill, ". . . the two conditions [autism and schizophrenia] are entirely unrelated. [Autism] . . . probably results from brain damage sustained before or during birth." In commenting on the fact that autism and childhood schizophrenia are sometimes equated, Morrison states, "The term childhood schizophrenia should be expunged from the dictionary; its use can be confusing to the physician, injurious to the patient, who may be inappropriately treated, and pejorative to the parent, who often finds himself unjustly scapegoated for the tragedy." Dr. Morrison, a psychiatrist in private practice and a clinical professor of psychiatry at the University of California at San Diego, was in perfect accord with Dr. Rimland on this point.

When Dr. Rimland heard about Georgie through Dr. Bérard, he wanted to know more about her. He was having trouble believing that she could be functioning so well if she had ever been truly autistic. He called me to tell me this (I was offended) and to ask me if I would mind filling out the diagnostic test known in the field as the "E-2 form" of the Autism Research Institute. This would enable him to determine exactly how autistic she had been if, in fact, she had been autistic at all. At this point I was so used to Georgie's miracle that I rarely thought about her early symptoms, but of course I was willing to take the test.

When it arrived a few days later, I was relieved to see that it was in the form of multiple-choice questions, which I hoped would jog my memory. They did, and although the extensive survey took hours to complete, it was a catharsis as the questions covered more ground than any medical form I'd ever completed. Finally, someone besides Bill, Georgie, and myself was going to know exactly what she'd been like in the first three years of her life.

When Rimland called to tell me that Georgie had received a score of plus nineteen, which put her in the category of classical early infantile autism, congenital and severe, with a negative prognosis, I felt vindicated. The last vestiges of guilt blew away like so much smoke. "You really ought to write a book," he said. "You are obligated to share her history with the autistic community." But I didn't feel the time was right, and Georgie agreed with me. Her story couldn't be known until she had graduated from college and was safely accepted and established at graduate school. Even then it would be risky, and would require all our strength to withstand the attention, skepticism, and negativity it would engender, and would only be worth it if we felt it would help dyslexic and autistic children.

Since Georgie had been on the Dean's List since the first marking period, she was able to take her junior year abroad in Italy. She spent an idyllic six months in Florence studying art history and going to the Uffizi Gallery. She came home fluent in Italian even though her roommates were American and all her courses were in English.

The art school Georgie attended was affiliated with a sizable university, and while she was away, a large ivory vellum envelope from the university arrived in the mail. Because it looked like an invitation and might require a fast answer (and because I was madly curious), I called her that night in Italy and asked her if she wanted me to open it and read it to her. It was an invitation to a banquet where she, along with several others, would receive the Regents Honor Award, the most prestigious academic award in the university, given to her for three years of outstanding work. Georgie was dumbfounded. She hadn't realized she was that good. She wouldn't be able to go because she would still be in Italy, and when I called the dean to tell her she said, "Don't worry about it, she'll probably win it again next year."

When she came home for the summer, she got a job working for a Connecticut fund-raising organization which lobbied for legislation benefitting the environment. Toxic waste sites in Connecticut were the focus, and Georgie went door to door for the rest of the summer asking for money. She worked on commission and did well, enjoying the contact with the people she met, and the fact that she was working for a good cause. Now she could add being a top-producing saleswoman to her list of accomplishments. (Needless to say, if I'd been told when she was three that years later she would be hired for a job like this, much less succeed at it, I would have said it was inconceivable.)

At Christmas during her senior year, I showed her an invitation to the annual Christmas party in the autistic unit at Bellevue. "Do you want to go?" I asked her. Georgie was up for it, although just barely, and a few days after Christmas we found ourselves driving down to New York.

Although she'd had her driver's license for years, she preferred that I drive into New York because it was notoriously difficult to find the way and her sense of direction was even worse than mine.

The unit had moved since we'd last been there, and the approach to it wasn't threatening and difficult anymore. A long, brightly lit corridor led to high-speed elevators, and the cavernous sky-lit day-room in which the party was held involved no running of the gauntlet through the disturbed children's ward. People were milling about, but there were few familiar faces. When we spotted Miss Dials, who had so ably herded us to and fro almost twenty years ago, she smiled in recognition and went to get Dr. Campbell.

Dr. Campbell greeted us with a smile of such genuine warmth that we were instantly receptive to her. She had mellowed, and looked relaxed and happy as she shook our hands and told us with great sincerity that she was extremely happy to see us. "Georgie," she said, "You look wonderful. How are you doing?" And she listened carefully as Georgie caught her up on her latest achievements. Then she turned to me and said, with a broad smile, "You are *relentless. That* is why she got well." I was taken aback and insisted that auditory training couldn't be discounted as the principle factor in Georgie's recovery. She didn't refute or pursue it, and our attention was drawn then by Georgie, who had wandered away to a table in the middle of the room. Emily was sitting there, Emily who had gone through the Bellevue Program with Georgie, and who had

roomed with her at Childville, who had always been higher functioning than Georgie, and whose mother I had envied for it. Now
she sat at the table in the middle of the room, wan and scattered,
twirling strands of her hair with both hands, her eyes cast down at
the empty table top. She spent her days in a day-care center for the
mentally handicapped. Georgie approached the table, her robust,
healthy looks in sharp contrast to Emily's pallid nervousness. As
Georgie sat down, Emily looked up and recognized her. "Oh hi,
Georgie," she said, glancing away and smiling a vague little smile,
her fingers moving in her hair.

"Hi, Emily," Georgie said with great tenderness.

When Georgie was in her senior year and took her graduate school
boards, her scores had risen considerably, and were now at least
respectable if not a true reflection of her abilities. Still, she didn't
think they were high enough for the top graduate school in her field.
But not only was she accepted, she was offered a scholarship as an
inducement to enroll.

Not long afterward, school was out. We moved Georgie out of
her dorm apartment and two days later drove back up with her for
graduation. It was a bright, hot May day, with the trees along the
Merritt Parkway exploding in pointilist patterns, all of us dressed
up and jubilant. "Georgie, how does it feel?" I asked. She leaned
forward in the seat, resting her chin close to my shoulder.

"Oh Mom, it feels great. It feels incredible."

Twelve hundred students were graduating from the university,
watched and applauded by four thousand spectators baking and
wilting in the hot sun. Georgie went to find her class and we staked
out wooden folding chairs for ourselves. They had been set out in
long rows on the grass, and their varnished seats were hot to the
touch. The School of Music orchestra expertly began to play the
Elgar processional music I loved. Peter wordlessly handed me his
handkerchief although he would be needing it too. When hundreds
of students began progressing down the three aisles, I was afraid I

would miss seeing Georgie, and said, "I'm going to go find her." I eased past ten sets of knees on my way to the aisle, and there she was, almost immediately. I was moved by the sight of her in her cap and gown. "It's so crowded, I was afraid we'd go through the whole thing without seeing you, there are so many people here." I hugged her, suddenly overcome with emotion, and then let her go, holding her away from me with pride. She gave me an appreciative look.

"Where are you supposed to be?" I asked.

"I don't know, I can't find anybody." Just then a group of professors marched by to the music and Georgie recognized one of them. She ran up to him. "Do you know where I'm supposed to be?"

"No, but just get in here with us and we'll find your classmates when we're up there." Georgie grinned sheepishly and eased into the line, the professors surrounding her in their splendid robes and kidding her about getting a fast doctorate. I'd probably be seeing her in a line like that again someday, legitimately.

After several speeches, and the conferring of the degrees, we headed in the direction of the art school for the main part of the ceremonies. This was where Georgie would actually get her diploma. Almost immediately we bumped into her, another amazing coincidence in this crowd, and we grouped around her excitedly. "Georgie, is it official now?"

"I guess technically, but I won't feel it's real until I get my diploma at the Art School."

There was an exhibit of the work of the graduating class mounted on the walls of the gallery in which the ceremony would take place. Georgie, who had by now joined the other seniors, had six vivid and dramatic prints on view, the largest grouping in the room, and a printmaking book of eight panels on a table. We found seats in the third row, and Peter looked over at Georgie's work on the wall. It was arresting even from forty feet away.

"They are professional," he said with respect. "They are unmistakably hers, aren't they?" Georgie won the award for outstanding student, and when she came up to receive it, her favorite teacher handed it to her and enveloped her in a hug. As we clapped and cheered, Sarah turned to Mark and said, "Does that mean she's the best?"

"Yes." He smiled down at her.

The class took up three rows facing us and now the students stood, one row at a time, to be called for the awarding of the diplomas. As Georgie came up, we heard "magna cum laude" ring out. As she took the diploma, and applause swept the room, she looked at us gratefully, and then over at Bill, who was standing against the wall by the door, applauding enthusiastically. When she went back to her chair, suddenly she seemed accomplished and confident. She had done it, it was real. When the ceremony was over, we found her and got into a family huddle, our arms tightly around each other in a circle as we congratulated her. Georgie looked at me.

"Oh, Mom," she said. "This is the happiest day of my life."

On June 7, 1988, three weeks after Georgie's graduation, I sat at the kitchen table reading the New York *Times*. I came across an article on the front page of the science section about autism, and my coffee got cold as I read about the extensive work of Dr. Courchesne (pronounced Coor-*shain*). Eric Courchesne, Ph.D., a researcher in the field of autism at Children's Hospital in San Diego, had published findings on the etiology of autism which agreed with Dr. Bérard's: that the center of the brain which filtered sensory input was where the problem lay. Through autopsies, abnormalities had been discerned which accounted for the excess, insufficient, and distorted stimuli experienced by autistic people.

A month later I was equally interested to see infrared photographs of the brain in an article entitled "The Anatomy of Autism" in July's *Life* magazine. The discrepancy in the autistic brain was clearly discernible. "This area regulates responses to outside stimuli like noises, heat and cold and may be involved in controlling some motion and memory." This would explain Georgie's extraordinary sense of balance, and why she never fell and hurt herself. And why she was able to stand up on the step stool in the kitchen so confidently, helping me make soufflés when she wasn't even two.

In an article on Dr. Courchesne's findings published in the May 26, 1988, issue of *New England Journal of Medicine*, more light was shed on autism as a developmental and neurobiological disorder. Autism as brain damage was becoming medical fact.

Several months later, Dr. Rimland informed me that he was going to Annecy to learn how to administer auditory training. Dr. Bérard was going to donate an "apparatus" to the Autism Research Institute in San Diego. After many years of routing people to France through Dr. Madel at the League for the Hard of Hearing in New York, auditory training was going to become available in this country. Possibly within a few years it would become routine in the treatment of those autistic and dyslexic children who could benefit.

Dr. Rimland is currently conducting a research project which will determine exactly how effective auditory training has been, although he says he has very little time these days because of all the attention he has received as a result of having been Dustin Hoffman's consultant for the movie *Rain Man*. Georgie and I were interested to see that the "Rain Man" only "decompensated" over airplanes, water rushing into the bathtub, and the smoke alarm. She said his reactions were sound-related, and she also said, interestingly, "Why did they have him move that way, in those little jerky motions? Autistic people don't move like that."

Georgie had a successful first year in graduate school, earning a 4.0 average for her second semester. Her second year hasn't been so easy, but she is excited about her future. Although she is committed to working as an artist, she wonders if she will someday work in the field of autism as well. She recently spent time with two autistic people who live nearby, and her relationship with them was uncanny. Barely verbal, and with no eye contact, both of them seemed to respond to her in a special way, as if they knew she understood them. She now wonders how she can be of the most help to them. She feels that allowing her story to be told is a beginning. ("But leave my love life out of it, okay, Mom?")

As for auditory training, she has always said it was the pivotal factor in her recovery. "Tell them I never would have made it without it, Mom. And the Lord. Don't forget to mention Him."

"And give Him the glory?"

"Right, Mom. And give Him the glory."

Afterword

Autism. The word is easy to say, and easy to spell, but that's where the easiness ends. No one, including me, understands autism at all well, and I have been studying it, intensively, for over three decades.

Researchers in many countries have established that autism occurs in about four or five children per ten thousand. In some cases, especially if the mother has had experience with other infants, the child's problems will be recognized soon after birth. In virtually all cases, the parents know there is something seriously wrong by the time the child is three. The overriding problem in autism is the child's failure to develop relationships with other people, including the child's own parents. The children are said to be living in a world of their own, or in a shell, or in a glass ball. *Autism*, from the Greek word for *self*, was applied to these children because their characteristic vacant, staring-into-space facial expression made them appear to be engaging in self-involved daydreaming. (The older dictionaries will even tell you that *autism* means *daydreaming*.) Half of the children do not speak. The other children do use words, but only in strange and stilted ways. Many autistic persons have savant-type mental abilities, but these skills are more impressive than useful.

Three out of four autistic children are boys, but—like everything else about autism—the reasons for that are poorly understood. Autistic children tend to be quite attractive and well developed physically. Their physical attractiveness is frequently commented upon, and is especially surprising, because virtually all other conditions characterized by severe "mental" problems also show a number of physical anomalies (stigmata).

As Annabel Stehli and many other thousands of mothers have learned, to their horror and dismay, the psychoanalysts chose to construe the child's *apparent* physical intactness, and *apparent* daydreaming, as evidence that autism was caused by emotional disturbance. That was proof, they concluded, very much to their economic advantage, that autistic children had no brain impairment but were simply normal children who had been so psychologically rejected and abused by their mothers that they chose to escape to a dreamworld. The psychoanalyst's job was to probe the mother's psyche to discover why she (supposedly) rejected the child, and to coax the child back to reality. This approach, which dominated American child psychiatry for close to half a century, and which persists in some European countries to this day, never did cure an autistic child, but it did make many child psychiatrists wealthy, wrecked many marriages, and caused some suicides. My book, *Infantile Autism* (published in 1964), was in part an exposé of the lack of scientific foundation for the psychogenic (blame the mother) view of autism. A 1979 national magazine article on autism said that 90 percent of the people in the field credited *Infantile Autism* with "blowing the 'refrigerator mother' theory to hell"—which is a good place for it.

While it is now generally accepted that autism is due to biological impairment, and is not caused by subtle emotional trauma, the exact site, nature, and cause of the impairment are as yet poorly understood. There is no treatment that is uniformly or fully effective. It *is* known that there are a number of different types of autism, and therefore different treatments, which need to be investigated. The Autism Research Institute (formerly the Institute for Child Behavior Research) in San Diego, which I direct, was established in 1967 as a central clearinghouse for information on autism. It is the only organization of its kind in the world. In its files are detailed case histories of over eleven thousand autistic children, from over forty countries. I established the Institute in response to the flood of mail and phone calls I received from parents worldwide after *Infantile Autism* was published. It was obvious to me that these parents, despite their having been browbeaten and demoralized by their contacts with child psychiatrists, were the source of immensely valuable information and ideas on what might have caused autism in their children, and on what treatments have been helpful, harmful, or useless. ARI compiles such information from parents and from the scientific and medical literature, analyzes it, and publishes the findings in various places, including our newsletter, the *Autism Research Review International*. Thus far, the most useful methods of treatment are behavior modification, which helps over 80 percent of the children, and high-dosage vitamin B6 and magnesium, shown in a number of published studies to be helpful in over 40 percent of the children.

My first letter from Annabel Stehli was one of about seven hundred I received that year from parents of autistic children. But her letter was unusual. Almost never do I get a letter saying an autistic child has recovered to the point of fitting smoothly into settings of normal people, and Annabel claimed her daughter was doing just that. I sent her our Diagnostic Checklist, asking for a great deal of detailed information about Georgie's early life. I expected to find that Georgie had never really been autistic, but had merely shown a few autistic-like symptoms, which she had outgrown. I was wrong. Georgie, to whom we assigned file number 9147, scored + 19 on our Diagnostic Checklist, in contrast to the average score of about 0 for children diagnosed as autistic by professionals around the world. (The scores, which may range from − 45 to + 45, are arrived at by a computer program which considers both positive and negative indications of autism.) Georgie's score placed her in the top 10 percent among autistic children, in terms of the number of autistic symptoms she had displayed in childhood.

Further, I learned she had spent several years as a patient in the unit for autistic children at Bellevue Hospital, under the care of my friend Dr. Magda Campbell, an internationally respected expert on childhood autism. A puzzling case!

Annabel wrote that Georgie's improvement had started with ten days of auditory treatment by Dr. Guy Bérard, a French hearing specialist whose clinic was in the little town of Annecy. I had met Dr. Bérard during his visit to the United States a few years earlier. Several U.S. parents who had been pleased with the improvement they claimed to have seen in their autistic children after Dr. Bérard's auditory training had written, urging that I meet him. Dr. Bérard, an intense, engaging fellow of great vivacity, explained how he had retrained from surgeon to hearing specialist as a result of what he had been told was his own inevitable deafness. He developed his auditory training method to treat his own hearing, then learned that it had many other applications, including, in some cases, autism.

Georgie's case was interesting, and Dr. Bérard's work proved to be interesting as well. But the world is full of interesting things and there are only twenty-four hours in a day. What *really* aroused my interest in Georgie's case, and Dr. Bérard's work, was a visit from Peter Stehli in 1987. Peter is a bright and friendly person, who made a very favorable impression on me. He told me with some pride about Georgie's accomplishments as a normal college student. "What percentage of her improvement would you attribute to the auditory training?" I asked, expecting an exaggerated estimate of perhaps 25 or 30 percent. Peter's reply astonished me: "One hundred percent." One hundred percent is a big number!

Could it be, I wondered, that in some cases of autism a treatment so simple as listening to electronically modified music for an hour a day for ten days could have so profound an effect?

I was very much aware that hypersensitive hearing is a serious problem for many autistic individuals. The Diagnostic Checklist I have been using since 1965 asks a number of questions about sound sensitivity and painful hearing. Parents' reports show that 43 percent of autistic boys and 34 percent of autistic girls "cover [their] ears at many sounds." Psychologist Carl Delacato has long advised parents that earplugs benefit many autistic children. Scientist Temple Grandin, a largely recovered autistic person, tells vividly in her book *Emergence* about the pain caused by her own hypersensitive hearing. Speech sounded to her "like an onrushing freight train." Philip Ney, a Canadian psychiatrist, had written several papers over a decade ago in which he proposed that hyperacute hearing might be a *cause*, and not just a *symptom*, of some forms of autism—but everyone, including me, had simply ignored his work. What was going on?

I must tell you that accepting Bérard's ideas was not easy for me. They ran counter to my preconceptions. But a researcher must be willing to abandon preconceptions, albeit with some discomfort. In my college science classes I was taught, and I later taught my students, what I call the brick wall theory of scientific progress: slowly, surely, systematically, in a very orderly fashion, each brick—each bit of new knowledge—is placed on the solid foundation of the bricks already in place. Thus, we are told, does science methodically advance. Nonsense! Nearly four decades as a full-time researcher has taught me that the crossword puzzle makes a much better model of how science really proceeds. Very often, finding the right answer in one corner will show that an answer already well established in some other corner is wrong, and needs to be erased. There is at least as much erasing of old answers as there is writing in of new ones. The more important the finding, the more likely it is to spring from the crossword puzzle, rather than the brick wall, process. Maybe some of my preconceptions of how autism must be treated needed to be erased. Perhaps a bit of humility, an acknowledging of ignorance, would be helpful.

Who would have thought that autism, in some cases, might be effectively treated by a device invented by an aging French surgeon to forestall his impending deafness? Yet, Georgie is by no means the only autistic person to have shown noteworthy improvement after Bérard's auditory training, although no other autistic person has improved nearly as much. In addition to the four or five parents who had urged me to see Bérard during his 1982 visit to the United

States, I have more recently been contacted by several additional U.S. parents who had heard of my interest in Bérard's work. They had previously taken their children to Annecy, and were so pleased that they wanted me to give their autistic children a second course of auditory training. I am, however, exclusively a researcher, and not a clinician, so I was unable to accommodate them. A recent mail survey of Dr. Bérard's patients has revealed many other parents of autistic children strongly supportive of the benefits of his work.

Dr. Bérard has recently retired and is no longer administering the auditory training he developed. However, his work is much too important to be abandoned. A number of his devices are in existence and other people will be taking up Bérard's work. A skilled electronics engineer with an autistic child is developing what he believes will be a much simpler, less expensive state-of-the-electronic-art version of the Bérard auditory training machine. His son had shown significant improvement after auditory training—improvement that evoked favorable comments from teachers who had no inkling that any form of treatment was being given.

Our institute in San Diego will monitor and periodically report new developments in auditory training, as it does with many other developments in the field of autism. Those interested in current information on Bérard's work or in learning more about other treatments for autism are invited to write (please do not telephone) the Autism Research Institute.

Bernard Rimland, Ph.D., Director
Autism Research Institute
4182 Adams Avenue, San Diego, CA 92116